RELATIONSHIPS TODAY
THE UPS & DOWNS AND THE UGLY TRUTH

WRITTEN BY

CHARLES LEE ROBINSON JR.

CHARLES LEE ROBINSON JR.

Copyright © 2023 Charles Lee Robinson Jr. All rights reserved.

No part of this book may be reproduced or transmitted in any form or by any means, graphic, electronic, or mechanical, including photocopying, recording, taping, or by any information storage retrieval without the permission, in writing, of the publisher. For more information, send an email to crobinson1968@yahoo.com

Casual Comfort Publication, LLC

USA / Florida

My website: amazon.com/author/robinsonc

CHARLES LEE ROBINSON JR.

FOLLOW ME

Facebook: Charles Lee Robinson Jr.

Twitter: @charliecivil

Instagram: Crobinson1968

Pinterest: crobinson1968

LinkedIn: Charles Robinson

Goodreads.com

YouTube Channel: Casual Comfort TV

@casualcomforttv7937

My website: amazon.com/author/robinsonc

CHARLES LEE ROBINSON JR.

RELATIONSHIPS TODAY

THE UPS & DOWNS AND THE UGLY TRUTH

WRITTEN BY

CHARLES LEE ROBINSON JR.

CHARLES LEE ROBINSON JR.

I've decided to put this book together of many different relationships and problems that go on daily. In doing so, I hope to shed some light on the many problems that men and women face today.

There will always be ups and downs in relationships and whether we want to agree with that, it's the ugly truth.

You must find that person who is equally yolked with you or who is very close to your personality. We all come with flaws, so there aren't any perfect relationships.

We must learn from our mistakes and so, I put together some relationships that you may be able to relate to.

Remember one thing: Be wise and careful when choosing a mate or being chosen by a mate.

CHARLES LEE ROBINSON JR.

I like to dedicate this book to all my fans and supporters and to everyone who's struggling with today's relationships and the problems that come with it!

CHARLES LEE ROBINSON JR.

This is a book with many different kinds of toxic

Relationships with a variety of bad endings!

CHARLES LEE ROBINSON JR.

RELATIONSHIPS TODAY
THE UPS & DOWNS AND THE UGLY TRUTH

WRITTEN BY

CHARLES LEE ROBINSON JR.

CHARLES LEE ROBINSON JR.

A Question?

This generation has changed the way relationships are supposed to work, will you change with them or will you live by the boundaries and standards to which you were taught or stand by?

TABLE OF CONTENTS

Single By Choice

Prologue

Chapter One – *It's all about me*

Chapter Two – *Don't start none, won't be none*

Chapter Three – *I mean what I say*

Chapter Four – *I am single by choice*

Chapter Five – *This can't be love*

What Motivates A Man To Love His Woman

Chapter One – *What I was taught as a boy.*

Chapter Two – *A failed marriage*

Chapter Three – *Moving on with my life.*

Chapter Four – *What motivates a man to love his woman.*

My Body Want Sex But My Heart Wants Love

Chapter One – *Talking shit with my girls*

Chapter Two – *Going on wild-ass dates*

Chapter Three – *Fucking the man of my dreams*

Chapter Four – *My body want sex but my heart wants* love

CHARLES LEE ROBINSON JR.

TABLE OF CONTENTS

Sometimes, A Man Just Wants Peace

Prologue

Chapter One – *Met her at Marco J's*

Chapter Two – *I let her move in too fast*

Chapter Three – *Taking my Kindness for weakness*

Chapter Four – *The communication part*

Chapter Five – *A man just wants his peace*

Just To Say I Got A Man

Chapter One – *I won't settle*

Chapter Two – *He treated me like shit*

Chapter Three – *He was cheating*

Chapter Four – *He started fighting me*

Chapter Five – *Gaining strength and confidence*

Chapter Six – *Loving on myself*

Chapter Seven – *Dating has changed*

Chapter Eight – *Having the conversation*

Chapter Nine – *The direction of our lives*

Chapter Ten – *Life will throw you a curveball*

Chapter Eleven – *Just to say I got a man*

CHARLES LEE ROBINSON JR.

TABLE OF CONTENT

Love Doesn't Have A Name

Prologue

Chapter One – *This is some mess*

Chapter Two – *Look at what you've done now*

Chapter Three – *I can't believe this here*

Friends With Benefits

Prologue

Chapter One – *I went out with the girls*

Chapter Two – *It went down*

Chapter Three – *He came over*

Chapter Four – *He gave me some good dick*

Chapter Five – *Round two in the shower*

Chapter Six – *He fucked me well*

Chapter Seven – *I had to tell my girls*

Chapter Eight – *Where the hell is Steven*

Chapter Nine – *We go got in the club*

Chapter Ten – *I talked to Steven*

Chapter Eleven – *Friends with benefits*

CHARLES LEE ROBINSON JR.

Chapter Twelve – *Chatting with my girls*

Chapter Thirteen – *I finally talked to Steven*

Chapter Fourteen – *He fucked me good*

Chapter Fifteen – *No hidden agenda*

CHARLES LEE ROBINSON JR.

SINGLE BY CHOICE

PROLOGUE

{MANY YEARS AGO}:

I walked into the kitchen where I saw my mother and Stepdad celebrating 15 years of marriage. "We made it, baby." Mother said. "We sure did," My Stepdad, Marion said. "What are your two celebrating and why are y'all so happy?" I asked. "Teresa, it's your Stepdad's and I, 15th anniversary." My Mother said. "Yes, we've been married ever since you were a little girl, truthfully you were a toddler, a cute baby," Marion said. "Aww, I was cute wasn't I, aww thank you, Marion," I said as I blushed.

"It has been a long, long time." Mother said. "You know we still have a lifetime to go, right?" Marion said. "I am with you until the end," Mother said with a huge smile on her face.

"Fifteen years, wow, that is a long time, so what's the key, how did you two manage to stay together so long?" I asked. "It wasn't easy at first because we had to learn from one another. "Mother said. "It wasn't an easy task, but once I came into your Mother's life and I saw your pretty face, I knew this is where I wanted to be," Marion said.

"After your father passed, (God rest his soul), I thought my life was over, it took many years for me to open up and heal, so when I met Marion, it just felt right, I fell in love with him, his words, his spirit, and his beautiful heart, he didn't have to come in here and take care of us, but he did, and to this day, I still believe God answered my prayers." Mother said.

"Did you fall in love at first sight, Marion?" I asked. "Of course, I did, just look at that pretty face, and that big behind let's not forget that, ha, ha," Marion said with laughter.

"Mother does have a big behind, I mean look at all that booty, ha, ha," I said as I giggled. "Will you two stop," Mother said as she started wiggling her big booty in circles.

"But, no, seriously though, I knew your Mother was something special when I met her, she was classy, beautiful, and had a big heart, how could a man not fall in love with her?" Marion said as he put his hands up in the air for an answer,

"It felt like Marion was sent from God, he was respectful and attentive, he listened to me and he always was open to communication, I knew he was the one for me, now look at us, fifteen years later, and that's why we are celebrating." Mother said. "Teresa, one day, you might meet a man, and hopefully he's a real good man," Marion said. "How will I know if he's a good man?" I asked. "You will know by the way he treats you, respects you, and protects you, always set boundaries for yourself and no matter what, never let any man cross them, if a man has a problem with your boundaries and he can't respect them, then he isn't the man for you," Marion said,

"A real man loves his woman, he makes sure she's okay, he makes sure she's secure and is stable, don't let any man tell you who you are and who you're not, and always know your worth." Mother said.

"That's a lot you guys are throwing at me," I said. "We know, but believe me, that's what kept Marion and me together this long." Mother said. "I admire, I adore, and most of all I respect your Mother, I have her back and she has mine, and that's how it should be, so when you get your man or your husband, you will see and know all the red flags," Marion said.

"What are red flags?" I asked. "What are red flags, girl, you have a lot to learn." Mother said. "What are they?" I asked. "Red flags are all the things a man does wrong to you in your life or what he isn't doing to make you elevate, do you understand?" Marion asked. "I think so, do you mean if he does things to keep us from being together as long as you two?" "Ha, ha, that could be it," Marion said as he laughed.

"That's it, Teresa, you are catching on quickly," Mother said and he and Marion started laughing.

"Well, I will let you two celebrate," I said. Mother and Marion poured a glass of wine and they started dancing while humming love songs. "Yuck, let me go, so you two can do grown people stuff." "If you don't know you better ask somebody." Mother said as she chuckled.

"Remember what I said, never let a man cross your boundaries and always respect yourself, know your worth and watch out for the red flags, etc.," Marion said as I walked out of the kitchen, "Good night you two," I said forcefully. I will never forget that conversation!

{MANY YEARS AGO}:
AFTER CHURCH

"Mother, where are we going, now?" I asked. "Church sure was good wasn't it?" Mother asked. "Yes, it was, I love Pastor Patterson," I said. "Me too, oh, we are going over to Sister Cynthia's house, they are having a Woman's retreat, and they said we can bring our daughters, so, I am taking you with me." Mother said. "With all those old ladies?" I asked with a frown on my face.

"Yes, with all those old ladies, they are all elders, and they can teach you a thing or two, all of them have been married for, twenty to fifty years or more." "Yeah, their old behinds need to sit down somewhere, did you see Sister Reynolds with that tight dress?" I said as I giggled. "Teresa." Mother yelled. "What?" I said. "Stop it, God said to come as you are, anyways, we are going to be chatting about men, and our marriages, there will be food and girls your age there."

"I don't want to be around those young girls, they are too fast, and I don't like that," I said. "I don't blame you, well you can stay with me and hang out with the old folks, ha, ha." Mother said. "I guess so," I said as we made our way to Sister Cynthia's house.

CHATTING WITH THE ELDERS

"Teresa, listen, girl, I have been married close to thirty years, and I tell you, a man should love you for you, no matter what." Sister Gaines said. "That's right, never let a man force himself or a relationship on you until you are ready, now me and my husband Georgie, have been married for sixteen years, and I tell you, it hasn't been all peaches and cream, but one thing I can tell you is, my husband respects me, get you a man who respects you, I mean when it's time." Sister Lacey said.

"Yeah, when it's time, she's too young now, but Teresa, listen to your elders now, those boys are always going to be there but those real men, they are hard to come by, so when you do get one hang on to him, you see that's why me and my hundred been married for twenty-five years, I got him and I latched on." Sister Cynthia said. "That ain't all you latched on to, ha, ha." Sister Monroe said and everybody started laughing. "Hush girl, hush, the babies in the room." Sister Cynthia said. "Y'all know I am just playing; I am just playing baby." Sister Monroe said. "It's all right, my baby has heard it all before." Mother said. "Well baby, everybody here is married except me, I am divorced, but one thing I've learned about a man is that if he loves you, no matter what, he will wait for you, he won't pressure you, and he will treat you like a Queen if he's interested in you, never let a man pressure you into a relationship or a marriage if you're not ready, stay single until you fill it in your soul that you are ready to settle down." Sister Cathey said.

"Girl, you can't give nobody any advice, your husband left you for a young girl, a tenderoni at that." Sister Monroe said and the room got quiet.

"You can say what you want to, it's his loss, not mine, and I can speak if I want to, that's why I am single and I am happy, some of you ladies are married and miserable, but me, I am happy and I am single by choice." Sister Cathey said and everyone got quiet.

You only heard whispers after that and all the Sisters split up and started talking among themselves. Sister Cathey, Sister Cynthia, and Mother kept talking to me. I must admit I learned a lot listening to those old girls that night. I think Sister Cathey, said something that all the other women didn't like, but I like what she said, "Don't let a man pressure you, or force you to do something unless you are ready to settle down," and she said, she is "Single by Choice", I like that, those are the words I will live by, I hope!

CHARLES LEE ROBINSON JR.

CHAPTER ONE

It's All About Me

{PRESENT TIME}:

After my husband and I divorced, I promised myself I would take time to love myself. Just because I want to remain single doesn't mean

I can't get a man, time after time, I have to keep telling my friends the same thing.

"Teresa, when are you going to get a man?" Tyronda said. "Yea, Tee, I am tired of seeing your ass couped up in this damn house watching the Golden Girls, get you a man," Iris said with laughter. "Listen, I am tired of yall telling me to get a man, I can get one if I want one, it ain't like a sister can't get one, see that's y'all problem, y'all always think you have to be in a relationship with someone to be happy," I said.

"You do, who told your lonely ass different?" Iris said. "Tell her something, Iris, she is missing out on that big thang," Tyronda said. "What big thang, I've been there and done that, dick doesn't mean you're in a relationship, hell the same dick you're riding, another chick could be riding his dick like a bicycle," I said.

"Your standards are too high, Teresa, quit playing," Tyronda said. "That's right Teresa, keep it up and you will be celibate for life," Iris said with laughter. "Ha, ha, I know that's right, I know you don't want to grow old alone?" Tyronda said. "Believe me, I won't be alone, right now, I want to find myself and just enjoy life, y'all can have that relationship shit, not me, not now," I said. "Let me get out of miss stale coochie's house," Iris said with a chuckle. "Ooh, girl, I know you didn't say that," Tyronda said with a smile on her face. "You know what, my coochie is still good and it doesn't have that many miles on it as yours do, now bye, get out my house, old rude asses," I said in laughter. "We are going, we are going, okay now, you need to get yourself some," Tyronda said. "And, you need to get your ass out of my house.," I said. "Now that's cold," Iris said as they both closed the door behind themselves.

I was glad when those girls left my house. They are always trying to tell me how to live my life when their lives aren't perfect. They are always having men's problems and then when they do, they come running to me so they can cry on my shoulder, hell no, that can't be me. I had my fair share of bullshit, now it's time for me. What part of being single by choice don't those whores understand?

CHAPTER TWO

Don't Start None, Won't Be None

Saturday night, I decided to go out with all my girls. Tamia, Tyronda, Iris, Stacey, and hot as Kiana. We had a ball, drinking, laughing, and dancing.

All night guys kept trying to talk to all of us, but I didn't pay them any mind. The girls entertained them, but I just kept dancing by myself. One of the guys talking to Kiana asked if I was into girls. "What did you say?" I asked as I overheard their conversation. "I asked were you okay." He said. "What's your name anyways?" I asked. "Teresa, don't," Kiana said softly. "Don't what, I heard what he asked you," I said. "Oh, girl, he was only joking," Iris said as she overheard the conversation. "What, what, what did I say, I am Joshua by the way." He said. "Well, Joshua, you can talk and play with them that way, but when you're messing with me, you're talking to a grown-ass woman, and I talk to whom I want to talk to, that doesn't mean that I am into women," I said.

"Teresa, chill out," Tyronda said. "Chill hell," I said. "Come on girl, let's get back out on this dance floor," Stacey said as she grabbed my hand. I pulled my hand away from hers. "Girl, it ain't that serious," Tyronda said. "Come here Teresa, and calm down, I'm sure he didn't mean anything by it," Iris said. "I didn't, I swear, I didn't, I am sorry Miss, your name is Teresa, right, I apologize," Joshua said. I looked him up and down; his expression told me he was probably telling the truth, so I accepted his apology and I got back on the dance floor with Iris and Tyronda and we kept dancing.

"Joshua, you better go, I will call you." "You do have my number right?" Kiana asked. "Got you, baby." He said. "Baby, damn, already?" Stacey said with an evil grin on her face. "That's right, he's going to find out that the coochie is 100 percent good," Kiana said with laughter.

"Hey, hey, what did I miss?" Tamia said as she came back from the bar with a pretty drink in her hand. "Nothing girl, put down your drink, and let's get our dance on," I said as we all danced in a circle.

I don't know what makes a man think he can just say anything to a woman. I don't know about my friends., but I am not one. He had the nerve to ask that of me, just because I wasn't paying his ass any attention. I still love my fine black men, I am just not ready for any relationships until I get my shit together mentally, and it is, what it is.

CHAPTER THREE

I Mean What I Say

"Hey, Teresa, this is Tyronda, what are you up to?" "Hey Tyronda, I am just sitting on my bed thinking about my life." "You're getting lonely, aren't you?" "No, I wouldn't say lonely, but sometimes, I just want somebody around, I mean a nice, strong, sexy, and loyal man." "I knew it, I knew it." "You knew what" "You are tired of being of not having your own man." "Sometimes, that may be true, but I just don't want to deal with all the bullshit, that's why, for now, I rather just stay to myself." "I understand that, I mean, I am seeing this guy name Tracey, and he just turned into a damn stalker." "See, that's exactly what I am talking about, nobody ain't got time for that shit." "Nope, not at all, and I am about to tell him to lose my damn number." "Tyronda, I don't blame you, that is a red flag, be smart, girl," I said.

"I agree, well listen, what are you doing this Friday?" "Nothing so far, why?" "Let's go bowling this weekend, are you down?" "Yes, sure, who's all going, just you and I?" "So far, maybe we can meet some good men there." "Ha, ha. At the bowling alley?" "Hell yeah, girl, there be some cuties there." "Damn, you are thirsty, aren't you?" "Hell no," Tyronda said with a sigh.

"Whatever, I will go with you, but I don't want to talk to anyone until I am ready, so please don't push me into anything, if anything happens, best believe it will be natural." "Natural my ass, you know you want some." "Whatever, yeah, right, you mean you want some, but you better sit your ass down before your stalker Tracey shows up." "Teresa, there ain't nobody thinking about Tracey, he better go about his business, I ain't scared of him, shit, he can't tell me what to do." "Yeah, yeah, whatever, I will see you this Friday," I said as I hung up the phone.

I don't understand why when you're not in a relationship, people think you should be in one like you can't just take a few steps back and get yourself together.

I am in no hurry to rush into anything, and then for some odd reason, people think that just because you are single you are lonely or always alone, that shit just pisses me off. I will never rush into another relationship again. It's on God's time, not my own.

FRIDAY came fast and I got myself dressed, I started to bring my gun, but I got my stuff out of my drawer just in case some drama or someone messed with me. I hurried and met Tyronda at the bowling alley. "Hey Teresa, I am glad you made it." "You thought I wasn't going to come, didn't you?" "No, I knew you were, I mean what else were you going to do, I know you don't have a date." "Girl, shut up, you don't know what I got, now, let's get these shoes so I can kick your ass on these lanes," I said as we went to stand in line.

"You know I was just playing right?" Tyronda said as I told the cashier what sizes of shoes we needed. "Oh, girl dead that shit, that talk to bother me none, you know me, no matter what, I am going to do me, and what no matter what you or anybody say or feel I should be with, it's going to be on God's time this time around, now lets bowl." "I hear you talking with your lonely and horny ass," Tyronda said in a whisper. "What?" I said. "Teresa, just bowl, I am going to kick your butt out here," Tyronda said with a cocky-ass attitude.

After I beat Tyronda's ass two games straight, we noticed two handsome guys a few lanes over staring at us. "Do you see them guys staring at us, Teresa?" "Yeah, I see them." "Ain't they cute?" She asked. "They are all right," I said as I walked up to the line in the lane.

I bowled a strike and I came back smiling and jumping up and down. "That was luck," Tyronda said. Just as she was about to bowl the two guys that were staring at us decided to walk our way.

"Hey, Teresa, look, I think they are coming over here," Tyronda said as she stuck her fingers in the bowling ball., and kept on bowling.

"Hello, ladies, how are you fine young ladies doing, I am Zack, and this is my homeboy Jeffrey." Tyronda smiled and she rolled her bowl and only knocked two pins down.

"Oh, it looks like somebody needs some help," Jeffrey said and we all started laughing. We introduced ourselves and the guys were actually cool. Tyronda kept trying to play matchmaker with Zack and I kept on pinching or so she would stop.

"So, are both of you ladies single?" Zack asked. "Yes, I am, are you?" I answered.

"What about you?" Jeffrey asked Tyronda. "Of course." She said. "Of course, that didn't sound too convincing," Jeffrey said. "I know right?" Zack said. "Ha, ha." I just laughed. "Yes, I am single, aren't I, Teresa?" Tyronda said as if to get me to co-sign for her. "Girl, don't ask me if you say so," I said.

"Teresa, so why are you single?" "I am single by choice, I am not ready for that commitment right now," I said. "Oh, you just got out of something?" Zack asked. "Yes, and I am not trying to jump back into something that isn't healthy for me," I said.

"It seems like you got your mind made up," Jeffrey added. "That's right, I am happy being single," I said. "I am not, I ain't going to lie," Tyronda said and we all stared at her.

"Maybe I can change your mind," Zack said. "Change my mind, didn't you just understand what I said, I am good, no disrespect but no thank you, we can be friends though," I said.

Zack acted like he didn't hear a word I said, he just kept trying. I laughed for a while and then it started getting annoying. I kept bowling while Tyronda and Jeffrey started hugging and kissing. I was disgusted because she just met this man and he already had his tongue down her throat. Now that's some nasty shit.

Soon as we started playing our so-called last game, Tyronda's friend Tracey came in and he snatched her ass up in front of everybody. I was ready to help her fight him but she told me she was all right as she walked out with him all embarrassed and shit.

"I thought your friend was single," Jeffrey said. "Hey, she said it, not me," I said. "Damn, that's messed up, she didn't have to lie, I bet he's going to give her the business when they get home," Zack said. "I am out of here, tell your girl she was wrong for that," Jeffrey said as he shook Zack's hand and started walking out. "You leave, man?"

Zack asked. "Yeah, I will call you later," Jeffrey said. "Well, I have to finish this last game and then I am leaving too," I said. "I guess I will stay with you," Zack said. "No, you better go, your friend just left you," I said. "No, it's cool, we drove our cars." He said. "Okay then, let me finish whooping on you," I said and we both laughed. "Yeah, right," Zack said as he chuckled.

We ended up playing another game, he beat me once and I beat him once. He kept talking to me about relationships, being my man, and what he would do for me. I kept trying to cut him off in mid-sentence, but he wouldn't take no for an answer.

"Let me turn my shoes in, I have to go, it was nice to meet you, and even better kicking your ass in bowling," I said. "Yeah, right, but for real, can I get your number?" "No, I don't think that's a good idea." "Can I walk you to your car?" "No, that's not a good idea either, it's been nice, I have to get home," I said as I handed the cashier my shoes and walked out the door.

"Hold up, can we just talk?" Zack asked again. "Don't you understand what no means, look, it was nice, like I said, now I have to go, maybe we will see each other next time," I said as I unlocked my car door.

"Look, you don't have to be that rude to me, I was nice to you," Zack said as he grabbed my arm and I sat down in my car. "Let my arm go, dammit," I said as I pulled out my can of pepper spray and I sprayed him in his eyes. After that all I heard was him crying and groaning in pain.

"Ah, ah, bitch, I can't believe you sprayed, I was only trying to talk to you." "I ain't your bitch, now, I told you no, too many damn times," I said as I pulled off in my car fast. I could see Zack falling and stumbling all over the parking lot as I left the bowling parking lot. He was lucky I decided not to bring my gun but instead bring my pepper spray because I probably would have shot his ass. He thought I was playing, but I was not!

CHAPTER FOUR

I Am Single By Choice

"Tyronda, why did you let that negro run you out of the bowling alley, I thought you were single, ha, ha?" I said.

"Girl, did you call me to make fun of me, because that shit wasn't funny, this dude is crazy, he thinks he can treat me any kind of way and I'm supposed to just take it and stay my ass home but to answer your question, I am ok, I am just pissed off, so what happened after I left, did you and that guy hit it off?" Tyronda asked.

"Girl, hell no, we didn't." "Y'all didn't, I thought y'all was hitting it off good?" "That; 's what you thought, I was only being nice."

"Damn, ok, did that guy Jeffrey ask about me?" "No, but he was pissed that you lied to him about being single, he didn't stay long, he left after you were hauled out." "Hauled out isn't the word, I thought he was going to kick my ass." "How did he find you anyway?" "That's a good, damn question, I don't know, he must have a monitor on my car or something." "Something, you see that's why I am staying single, these negroes are crazy and some of them think you are their property, I can't tolerate that shit."

"It isn't that bad, but Tracey must be a damn detective." "So, what did he say?" "He said he saw my car there and he came in and saw us talking to those men and it made him jealous." "If you ask me, that sounds like a bunch of bullshit, but you have to be more careful, you could've gotten that guy killed." "Tracey won't hurt a fly." "That's what you think, I saw the way he grabbed your ass by the arm and out of that bowling alley like you was a bag of garbage, ha, ha, I was like damn, she's single my ass."

"Ha, ha, very funny, but I will have to be more careful next time." Next time? There won't be a next time with me hanging with your riding the fence ass, you're either with or not with that crazy ass man, I just don't understand y'all confused assess."

"Teresa, I am not confused." "Tyronda, you are a damn lie, I mean look, just admit it." I ain't admitting shit, Tracey knows what's good for him, and he better not lay his hands on me." "If you keep messing around that's exactly what he's going to do, you can't keep playing with people's feelings, just let the man go if you don't want him."

"Yeah, you are right about that, this shit is giving me too many headaches." "I know it is and that's exactly why I am still single because I can do bad by myself and hell, I can give myself headaches, I don't need a man to do that."

"You do have a point there, so tell me what happened with you and that guy, because you did say hell no to y'all not hitting to off." "Let me tell you, girl, you are going to laugh at this shit here." "What, what, tell me, tell me, what happened?"

"At first. It was all good, we even played a couple more games after you and that guy Jeffrey left, then we kept pestering me about relationships and he wants to get to know me."

"And, what's wrong with that?" "I told him like I told you, I am not ready for all that, I am doing me, I am getting to know me again and at this point in my life, I just want to be single."

"What happened then?" "He kept trying, so I told him it was time for me to leave, and so, he followed, me out to my car and just as I was going to sit in my driver's seat, he grabbed my arm and insisted that I give him a chance." "No," "Yes, and before I knew it, I pepper-sprayed his ass. "Ha, ha, "you did what, oh, God, your ass is crazy, and what did he do?" "What do you mean what did he do, he couldn't do shit, because his eyes were burning, he was in too much pain, I just started my car and I hauled ass."

"Oh my God, you are crazy, now we can't go back to that bowling alley." So, what, he shouldn't grab my arm like that, that's his fault." "Ha, ha, I guess he should've listened to your crazy ass." "He sure should've, because when I pulled off, I could hear him screaming like a little bitch, my eyes, my eyes, you dirty bitch, he said over and over, I think he even started crying." "Ha, ha, that shit burned his eyes, I bet, damn that's crazy, I couldn't have done anything like that."

"Hell, he got lucky because I started to take my damn gun but I decided to leave it at home, these men need to learn that no means no." "You tried to tell him." "You did, but Teresa, somewhere down the line you have to find yourself a man." "When God brings a man into my life but until then, I am staying single, I mean, it isn't like I can't get a man, I am single by choice, and that's it." "I hear you girl, well let me get off this phone, Tracey and I need to talk." "Okay, Tyronda, good luck girl, now don't get your light ass slung like garbage, ha, ha, that was so funny." "Ha, ha, no that wasn't, I won't, Tracey knows better, okay talk to you later, Teresa. "Okay, he knows better, bye girl, and good luck, chat later," I said as I hung up the phone.

Some of these women don't get it, but I do and I am very happy being by myself. I have been through so much trauma from failed relationships and I just don't want the aggravation anymore, and on top of that being married to an asshole took me over my boiling point.

Some women are forced to be single because we have little to no one to choose from who is actually worth or ready to be serious, so they rather stay single, but me, it's my choice until my body, mind, and soul line up to what I feel is real, to what I feel is comfortable and natural. When it's time, I will know because God will let me know.

THE END!!!

CHARLES LEE ROBINSON JR.

WHAT MOTIVATES A MAN TO LOVE HIS WOMAN

CHAPTER ONE

What I Was Taught As A Boy

As a young man, I was taught by my elders how to treat a woman. The very first person I talked to was my Mother. She constantly explained that I needed to learn how to treat a lady.

She would explain to me that a man had to make a woman feel secure and stable. I asked her why, and she said, "It makes a woman put her trust in you. I understood what she was saying, not knowing I would one day apply those teachings to my life.

The next person to enlighten me was my Father. He and Mom had been married for twenty years and I often asked him how they managed to stay together so long.

He always said, "I didn't want to live without your mother, she was always a good woman to me, and once you feel that in your heart and soul, never let that woman go."

"What if I stay loyal and true to her but she doesn't do the same?" I asked. "It's up to you what you will take from a woman, if you feel deep down that she's worth the fight then fight it out and stay with her through thick and thin," Dad said.

I always remember those talks with them. I knew relationships wouldn't be easy, but I was taught to love and take care of my woman no matter what.

My Granddad was also in my ear about relationships. He and my grandmother were together for over 40 years, and they loved each other to pieces.

"Neil, when you get you a woman, you better treat her right and communicate with her at all times, women love a man who can talk about things, hell they love to talk about anything." He said.

"You and Grandma truly love each other to be together that long Granddad," I said.

"She is my everything and I make sure she knows that at all times." He said. "How do you do that?" "It's easy, I tell her and show her daily."

"Don't you ever get tired?" I asked. "I never get tired, and it never gets old, I learned a long time ago to see things from a woman's perspective, you know, learn how to walk in her shoes, it'll take you a long way."

"How can I do that Granddad?" "Learn your woman, and you will know when she's happy or sad without her even telling you." He said.

Those conversations with my Grandad were most entertaining, but I must say, I learned a lot about women from him. Then there were the lessons from Grandma, and those conversations were life-changing for me as a young man.

Grandma would say, "Neil, no relationship will ever be perfect but it's up to you to be perfect while you're in it." It confused me a bit. "Grandma, I don't understand that, speak in English," I said. "Boy, if you don't shut up and listen, what I am trying to say is, no matter what that person does, you try to put in the best you have to offer and if they fail on their part, it doesn't mean you have to follow them, you know like, tit for tat?" "You mean to do my best and if the relationship falls short, I won't be the blame because I did all I could to make it work?" "That's exactly what I was saying, and always respect your woman and know that we all have faults, some things you can overlook, you know some little things, but big things, you have to decide if you want to stay around for all that drama." She said. "Did you and Grandad have a perfect marriage, and without drama?" "Excuse, my, French,

Hell no, we had ups and downs but once we took the time to learn one another, things got easier with time."

"Okay, I see, so sometimes, you need to have patience because things could change and get better?" "Sometimes, but grandson, please don't be nobody's fool." "I won't Grandma, I won't," "Good, and always remember what I taught you." She said.

I learned a lot from my family, and those are the tools that I apply to my life in every situation, I pray in time they work out.

CHAPTER TWO

A Failed Marriage

"Neil, I've told you over and over again that I want a damn divorce," Quila said. "But, why, I have been nothing but good to you, why can't we work this out, you're my wife for God's sake." "Your wife, your wife, that's only on paper, look, Neil, you are a nice man, but I don't love you anymore."

"Why, but why, what have I done to you, I've always treated you with respect and I have done everything for you." "Neil, honey, it's not you, it's me, I just think you're too nice." "Too nice, now that doesn't make any sense." "You are a pushover and I don't like that."

"I am not a pushover, I was just taught to treat a woman the right way, and I am sorry you weren't raised to know the importance of love and family." "What, let me get the hell out of this house, I want a divorce," Quila said as she walked out of the door.

I tried to talk to Quila about working things out, but she was so eager to just call it quits.

"Quila, can we please try, can we go get counseling or something?" "I don't need counseling; I just don't want to be with you." "Baby, what else do I have to do, I didn't marry you to just give up on us." "You need to sign these divorce papers and let me go on with my life."

Quila didn't want to stay in the marriage, no matter what I said or tried to do. I don't know what I did to make her like this. She wouldn't tell me, all she kept saying was that I was a nice man, but shouldn't that have been enough for her to want to try and fix the marriage?

Quila stopped coming home every night and she would just waltz in any time she wanted to and when I asked her where she had been, she would curse me out. I let her disrespect me over and over again and I still kept on trying to keep my wife and our marriage.

She meant everything to me, but nothing I said got through to her. I didn't know what to do, so I called my Dad and told him what was happening. I was hoping he would give me some good advice.

"Son, listen, you can't make a woman stay if she wants to go." "But you taught me to fight for the woman I love." "Yes, I did, but in this case, it sounds like your wife doesn't love you or respect you, for instance with your mother, she and I loved each other, we were not perfect, and we both knew that, and that's what helped us get through everything that we did." "So, what you are saying is to just let my wife go?" "What I am saying is, it doesn't sound like she's your wife anymore, let her go, or you might suffer some painful consequences later on down the line." "But I love her Dad, do you remember the conversation we had many years ago and you said to me, ", "I didn't want to live without your mother, she was always a good woman to me, and once you feel that in your heart and soul, never let that woman go."

"Yes, I do, Son, but your wife isn't your mother, the difference here, again, is your mother had the same love for me that I had for her, your wife doesn't love you, I mean she can't if she wants to end your marriage without a cause."

"Yeah, she doesn't have a good reason to not love me and to keep this marriage because I have been nothing but good to that woman."

"I know you have a Son; do you remember when you asked me, "What if I stay loyal and true to her but she doesn't do the same?" "Yes, I do Dad, and?" I said to you, "It's up to you, what you will take from a woman, if you feel deep down that she's worth the fight then fight it out and stay with her through thick and thin,"

"Fight it out through thick and thin is what I am doing Dad." I know you are, but dammit, you can't be the only one that's doing the fighting, Son." Dad said this force.

After that talk with Dad, I guess you can say, I realized that I should let Quila and the marriage go. I left work early with the divorce papers in my hand and headed home to tell Quilla I was giving her what she wanted.

As I entered our home, I caught Quilla and some man fucking in our bed. My first thought was to kill both of them, but I shot the divorce papers at their naked asses, and I said, "Now y'all can have each other, get the fuck out of my house now, before I do something that we will all regret," I walked out of the house, and I jumped in my car.

My heart had never been hurt so badly. I tried to hold in the pain, but the tears started getting the best of me. I am a man, and she just tried to kill my manhood, and my pride.

All I ever wanted was a marriage that would last a lifetime, like my parents and grandparents, but this is a different time and people don't want the same thing.

Even though I was hurt, I didn't leave bitter, because I knew one day, I would find the right woman to love.

CHAPTER THREE

Moving On With My Life

I am not going to lie, being a divorced man was kind of strange to me at first. Even though some of my friends were married and some were single, I always found myself hanging around the married guys most.

My boy Gary Wollack was one of those guys because he and his wife had been through hell and back and they still managed to stay together fourteen years.

"Neil, you know one day, you will find your soulmate, believe me, she's out there, just look at Yvonne and me, we are still making it work."

"I know you are Gary, but some women don't want to put that work in. Quilla did me dirty and she said I was too nice; I don't understand that."

"Neither do I, Some women have agendas just like some guys do, but you must move on with your life, and I guarantee you will find that right woman one day," Gary said.

Then there was my homeboy, Boris Alexander. He and his wife were together for a little under five years and they both caught each other cheating and they both stayed married and still trying to make it work.

"Man, how could you stay with your wife Shonell after she cheated on you?" I asked.

"That shit was hard but hell I cheated first, and she took me back so why can't I take her back, that's how I looked at it."

"That's true, but don't you ever think about it?" "Hell yeah, I think about it, but I also think about my actions that led me to do what

I did, the bottom line is that we are all at fault, Shonell realized it and I realized it, she knows why I did what I did, but that's another story."

"I understand that I was trying to fix things with my ex-wife, but she didn't want that."

"Every woman isn't the same, don't let her bad judgment cloud your mind, there are good wifey-material women out here, just take your time, live right and God will send you the right one, trust me."

I also talked to my friend Sheldon Bradley and he and his wife were only married for two and a half years.

"Neil, listen, don't trust these women, they are not shit and they ain't no good, they lie, cheat, and never want to be held accountable for their damn actions."

"Man, how could you say that when you are still married to Natasha?"

"I still don't trust her, I still don't trust, matter a fact, I trust her as far as I can throw her, and with that big ass she got, it isn't very far."

"Ha, ha, damn man, you are bitter." "Bitter, how am I bitter, I am only telling the truth, Neil, and you know I am, don't you?"

"Men and women at some point in their life can't be trusted, it's all about building up that maturity level and knowing who you are, you're just bitter, but I don't understand because you are married."

"My wife married; I'm not married." "What, damn, you are crazy as hell, I can't believe you."

"Why you can't, didn't your wife cheat on you?" "Yes, she did." "So, what that tells you?" "She wasn't used to a real man loving her." "Hell knaw, she ain't no damn good, she lied to you, she cheated on you, and if you trust another woman. Man, hey, that's your heart, but they won't break mine no more."

"Ha, ha, you bitter ass." "I am not like I said, women do shit too and they always bash men, but they never hold themselves accountable for what they do, they blame men for the same shit that that they do, and they are quick to get on each other's side, but if men get on each other's side, we don't know what we are talking about, right?"

"I guess that happens sometimes, like when I try to give my female friends advice, they always look at it like I am only speaking for me and no other men, but that doesn't make them all bad," I said.

"Okay, okay, you play the big dummy, Fred Sandford ass dude, I bet I won't." "But man, you're married, I can't believe you. "Believe it," Sheldon said as he started breathing heavily.

One thing about Sheldon, he keeps it real, but he and his wife are perfect for each other. I just can't live my life feeling like all women are the same just like women shouldn't believe that all men are the same.

Either way, I took something from all my friend's experiences, and I began to heal. I went on to live my life as I saw fit, and my mind always stayed on the positive things in life, at the top of my list was finding a woman who wants to be loved.

In the process of moving on with my life, from time to time I would get advice from my Mother. My Mother always knew the right things to say to me.

"Hey Neil, how's my Son?" "I am okay Mother; I am just moving on with my life." "And, so you should, look, don't come down on yourself, you know in your heart and soul you did your best, and I know you did,"

"I did Mother, but that wasn't good enough." "That's nonsense, it wasn't good enough, it just wasn't the right woman appreciating it, remember that, never let anyone keep you from being you, I've taught you well, so keep your head up and man up, let God do the rest."

"Yeah, I guess, I still remember when you told me, "A man had to make a woman feel secure and stable, I asked you why and you said, "It makes a woman put her trust in you, but what I've found out is that's not all women." "That is true, but don't let that dark cloud take away your shine, you are a good man, and sooner or later a good woman will see that, one thing that I ask you, Son." "What, Mother?" "Just don't give up, the right woman is out there, but take your time in finding her." "Okay, Mother."

CHARLES LEE ROBINSON JR.

My mother always knew the right things to say to me and that gave me hope.

CHAPTER FOUR

What Motivates A Man To Love His Woman?

It took me so many years to heal from the pain of my past relationships and my failed marriage. There were days when I felt like giving up, but why would I give up on love?

I realized that everyone has their part in a bad breakup. Maybe I was too nice, and maybe I was a pushover, but I thought I was doing the right thing for my wife and our marriage.

With healing, God helped me stand back upright. I walked and ran up Cobbs Hill Trails in Rochester, New York daily, just washing all the bad memories away.

It is a slow process, but I was willing to go the extra mile. I am blessed to be the man that I am and with God's strength, I will never change.

As I made it to the top of the hill to the Rochester Reservoir, I received a phone call from my Grandparents. I had on a grey hoodie and white shirt, and I was soaked in sweat.

"Hello," I said while breathing heavily and barely able to catch my breath. "Hey Neil, your Grandma, and your Grandad are here with me, we just called to check in with you, are you okay?"

"I am doing just fine, thanks," I said. "Hey boy, you sound out of breath, what are you doing, kissing some girl," Granddad said in the background.

"Don't I wish, maybe one day," I said. "Neil don't rush it, I know you're still hurt over the divorce and everything, but just let God work in your life, he works out all kinds of miracles," Grandma said.

"I am not rushing, I was getting my walk in at the trails," I said. "Well, that's good, keep your head up at all times, because you represent our family, and our family has always had strong and proud men," Granddad said.

"So, I hear, but I am not so sure about the women these days Granddad, they are not like the women in your days," I said.

"What's so different?" Grandma asked. "They don't want to stay in relationships and have commitments," I said. "I am sure that isn't true, you can't speak for every individual, you just met a bad one," Grandma said. "Hell, I did that before," Grandad shouted. "What?" Grandma said. "Oh, not you baby, I am talking about before you, way, way, way, way, before you," Granddad said with a slick tongue.

"All right now Grandad, Grandma going to get you, ha, ha." "He knows, he knows, you don't have to tell him," Grandma said as she giggled. "Anyways, as I was saying," Granddad said with sarcasm. "What's up Granddad, as you were saying," I said. "Do you remember what I told you a long time ago?" "You told me a lot of things," I said.

"Roland, just say what you have to say, that boy doesn't remember," Grandma said. "Remember I told you, "Learn your woman, and you will know when she's happy or sad without her even telling you, now, did you do that, or did you just jump head over heels for that girl?"

"I guess, I mean I thought I learned her," I said. "You thought and you guess, now you know that don't make no damn sense," Granddad said as he was scolding me. "Roland, take it easy on my Grandson, now." "Liz, he's a grown man now, let us men talk for a minute, please, you notice how I said please, now didn't you? "Granddad said.

"Please," Grandma said. "Okay now, you getting Grandma upset," I said. "She is not upset; she isn't upset because she knows I am telling you the truth and I come with facts."

True, true, I said. "Hurry up and get your point across, Roland," Grandma said.

Okay. Okay, now do you also remember when I said, "When you get you a woman, you better treat her right and communicate with her at all times, women love a man who can talk about things, hell they love to talk about anything."

"Yes, I do remember that, and I tried to do just that, but she wasn't hearing none of that," I said.

"Well, maybe you just didn't have the right girl, I guess it's time to trade her in, ha, ha," Granddad said with laughter.

"It's too late, she's already old news," I said. "That's good, now let me go in here and watch some wrestling," Granddad said. "He loves his wrestling, he even got me hooked on that fake junk, oops, don't tell him I said wrestling was fake, that fool would have a fit, let's forget I said that ha, ha," Grandma said as she giggled.

"It's fake Grandma, ha, ha, you two are hilarious, I just love it," I said as I couldn't stop laughing at how they interacted together. All I could do was wish I had love like this!

"Neil, now listen to your Grandma, I know all your life we have taught you and prepared you to be a good man, but being a good man also comes with making better decisions and that means even when it comes to picking a woman."

"I know Grandma, I've made bad choices, but I am ready for that special lady, but I won't rush it. "You better not, some of these young girls don't know how to receive a good man, that's all."

"I tried my best to be a perfect husband, Grandma." "I told you a long time ago that, "No relationship will ever be perfect but it's up to you to be perfect while you're in it."

"I do remember that, and I did my best," I said. "Well, that's all you could do, and don't ever beat yourself up about it, you're a good man, and one day you will find the right one."

"I hope I won't be too old and half-dead by then." "Stop it, your time will come, and you will make a great husband again, maybe this time you will be appreciated." That's sweet, thank you, Grandma." "You are welcomed, now there's no need to hold you up any longer, we love you and we hope the best for you, but don't ever be a woman's doormat, you deserve better, after all, you are a Richardson and don't you ever forget it, now let God guide you through, I will talk to you later, I love you, Grandson." "I love you too, Grandma," I said as I hung up the phone. As I stood on top of the hill glaring at the sun while all the sweat fell down my face, I began to reflect on my failed relationships, my failed marriage, and all the things that my family taught me.

I finally concluded that what motivates a man can be many things, God is most important, but other than that what motivates a man to love his woman is her loving him back the same.

I have come to terms with myself even though I am still in the healing process. Being the man that I am, I will never change because this is how I was raised, to love, cherish, respect, and be loyal to one woman.

THE END!!!

CHARLES LEE ROBINSON JR.

MY BODY WANT SEX BUT MY MIND WANTS LOVE

CHAPTER ONE

Talking Shit With My Girls

"Hey Latisha, I am sorry I am late, did you buy anything in the mall yet?" "No, Loraine, I was waiting on you, Marcella, Giovanni,' now you're here, where are those hoes?" "Girl, you are crazy as hell," Latisha said.

"Hey girls, are you all talking about us?" Marcella and Giovanni's asked as they walked up." "No, we weren't," Latisha said. "Yes, I was,

Latisha might be scared but y'all hoes know I'm not scared, now why are yall always late every time, I set up a time to meet, are you out here sucking dick, fucking a sugar daddy or what?" I asked.

"Loraine, you are off the chains, anyways, I am here now, I'm not always late, am I?" Marcella asked with a curious look on her face. "Hell yeah, I just fucked a sugar daddy, hell my mortgage needed to be paid, I guess it was fucking, I mean the shit only lasted two minutes," Giovanni said, and we busted out laughing.

"Girl, let me get this right, Giovanni,' you got a sugar daddy, and he paid your mortgage?" I asked. "That's right bitches." Giovanni said. "How much is your mortgage?" I asked. "My mortgage is $1500 a month," Giovanni said. "Then what the fuck am I doing wrong?" I asked. "But didn't you say he only fucked you for two minutes?" Latisha asked. "That's it, hell it took him almost a minute to get that old dick up, with the help of Viagra that is," Giovanni said as she chuckled. "He kind of fucked you for only two minutes and he paid you $1500 hundred for your mortgage, damn, I need me a sugar daddy too, where the hell did you find his old ass at?" Marcella asked with a puzzled look on her face.

"Never mind, never mind, I don't want to hear none of this shit anymore, I want to go shopping," I said. "Loraine don't be hating on me girl, you need to find yourself an old ass man too," Giovanni said. "Hell no, I ain't fucking or half fucking an old ass man, I will save my good ass pussy for a real man," I said. "Where do you find them in the Salvation Army?" Latisha said as she chuckled. "You know you need some dick so stop being so extra special, you know that stale pussy got cobwebs," Marcella said. "Fuck you, I don't care what y'all talking about, I ain't fucking no old man for money, truthfully, I don't think no man is worthy of getting some of this," I said. "Don't knock it to you try it," Latisha said. "So, all you hoes fucking old ass men?" I asked. "I tried it, but I couldn't get passed the time when I was about to fuck old man, Henry," Latisha said. "And, what happened?" Marcella asked. "Nothing, that dude pulled out a box of Magnums and it said extra-large condoms," Latisha said. "So, what's wrong with that?" I asked. "Well, his dick was too little to fit in the extra-large condemn," Latisha said, and we all started crying in laughter. "What the hell, little pee wee bit off more than he can chew, see that's why I ain't fucking with no shriveled-up dick O.G.," I said. "Damn his dick was too little for a magnum, ooh girl, I bet you ran out of there, didn't you?" Marcella asked. "Not fast enough, I made sure he gave me some money to pay my car note first, and then I was ass out of there," Latisha said, and we started laughing harder. "Listen, right now, I don't want a man, I want to stay single, plus love is overrated as fuck." I said. "Loraine, you're just saying that because you haven't met the right man," Marcella said. "She just needs a man to knock those old cobwebs off that pussy, that's all," Giovanni said. "As I said, I don't want a man, and no one ain't knocking shit off me, hoes, my pussy too good for that," I said. "Wait until you meet the right one, he's going to tear that ass up." Latisha said." "That will happen will hell freezes over, let's stop talking, and let's go shopping," I said. "Now you are talking my language." Giovanni said." "Yes, shopping is therapy," Marcella said.

As we walked into the mall, Giovanni walked up to me and whispered, "You better get yourself a sugar daddy." "Fuck no, and fuck you, who's next," I said, and she started laughing. "Aww, girl go get yourself some." Latisha said." Girl shut up." I said as we headed to find something in the mall.

CHARLES LEE ROBINSON JR.

CHAPTER TWO

Going On Wild-Ass Dates

After listening to my girls, I decided to start dating. I got tired of them ragging on me. It was starting to piss me off. They acted like I should be desperate or something. One thing you must know about Loraine Simmons is that I can get a man if I want to and I ain't fucking no old ass man.

One day I met this nice guy at the grocery store. He snuck up behind me while I was reaching for some boxes of cereal and he asked me did I needed help and of course, I said yes.

We chatted for a while as I continued to grocery shop. He sounded like a well-rounded guy, and he had himself together, so I gave him my number as we left the parking lot.

He said his name was Maserati, or Maz for short. It kind of threw me off at first because who's damn momma would name their son after a car? Well, the truth came out, that was just his street name, and that's what his friends called him. His real name was Maximus, but I do not like that name either, so I just called him Max. We conversed for weeks before we went out on a date.

Finally, the night came, and we met at a restaurant in a secluded location near the boardwalk. As we sat down for dinner we began talking

"Girl, you look tasty as fuck, I love that dress, but next time wear a shorter one." He said.

"Say what, what did you say?" "You heard me, that ass looks good, can I taste you right now?" "Max, where is all this coming from?" "Stop playing, you know I want to taste you, I want to lick your ass and everything, you know you want this, you probably haven't had any dick in years." He said with a cocky-ass attitude. Before I knew it, I grabbed the pitcher of water on the table that was filled with lemons and I drenched his horny ass and I said, "You don't even know me that well to eat my pussy or my ass, I thought you were a good guy but that was just your representer, I'm out of here, you nasty ass jerk, you won't be eating shit over here," I said as I walked out of the restaurant. "You bitch, you know you want this, I can't believe you did this shit." He yelled. "Your momma is a bitch for having you, now eat that, bitch." I yelled as I made my way to the car.

"Damn, so you left him at the restaurant drenched?" Latisha asked as I was telling her the story over the phone. "Yes, he had lemons all on the top of his damn head. "He wanted to eat all those cobwebs out of that pussy." she said in laughter. "Bitch, shut up, why are men so immature, they don't even know a bitch and they want to dive straight down into your legs, that's a big turn-off," I said. "Shit, no it ain't, if they want to eat, I am spreading like a bald eagle and then I am grabbing their head and mushing it harder, I bet I get my nut, ha, ha," Latisha said as she laughed. "You know what you're a nasty, dumb, bitch, I know my worth." "Fuck your worth, I am, talking about this clitoris wrapped around his lips." She said while laughing. "It's not funny, I hate dating, most of these men just want someone to fuck, and I am at the age where I want more than that," I said. "Damn, don't get so serious, one day you will find Mr. Right." "I don't think so, I am tired of dating, most of these men don't know what the hell they want." "Yes, they do, they want to wax them cobwebs out of that pussy, ha, ha," Latisha said with laughter again. "You're dumb bitch, bye," I said as I hung up the phone.

I called my other girls, and they were all clowning me and telling me not to give up. I tried dating a few more times. I dated this guy named Scooter; his real name was Raphael. He was cool but all he talked about was himself and he talked about his package a lot, which turned me off.

After that, I stayed to myself. I couldn't take any more bullshit that these men were trying to put out. I do not entertain bullshit. Why can't I find someone nice and made for me? Maybe I should just be like them hoes, they get everything they want. But I know deep down, that wasn't me, so I prayed about it and I just stayed patient.

CHAPTER THREE

Fucking The Man Of My Dreams

I dated off and on for over a year and I finally met a nice guy whom I met at the Home Depot while buying some things for my home. His name was Kenneth Grant.

He helped pick out some cabinets for my kitchen. He was a real gentleman; he even carried all my things out to my SUV. I was reluctant at first to give him my phone number because I was fed up with men and their lies. Something inside of me told me he was different. I guess it was my woman's intuition.

We exchanged numbers after he kept trying to persuade me, so I gave in. He called me before I even made home from the store. We stayed on the phone that entire evening.

His conversation was soothing, I loved the tone of his voice and the way he was very passionate about what he believed in. I was immediately attracted to him. I guess you can say the chemistry was good. I couldn't wait to see him after talking for weeks on the phone.

We met out at the Villa, we had drinks, and we went walking in the park. I felt so comfortable with him, it felt like I had known him for years. I was instantly drawn to him the more we spent time together.

It got to the point that every time I spoke to him or saw him, I would get a little horny. I started sizing him up and I got a little touchy-feely. It was the best time I had in years. Up until then, I had kept him a secret from my family and friends. I did not want to make a fool of myself this time, so I waited until we had gotten close.

My girls couldn't believe it when I told them about him. My mother said I was lying, and I hadn't met anybody, so I just left it at that. My girls were so eager to meet him, but I didn't think it was time to meet him face to face until he and I made things official.

I hid Kenneth's ass for almost six months from everyone. We were still going strong, and I truly started caring for him. He had a good heart and a beautiful shit, we had so much in common that it was scary at times. I knew I couldn't let a fine-ass man like Kenneth get away, so as the chips fell in place, we became intimate.

After we made a mess of each other, we lay on the bed, we cuddled, and we laughed. The sex was so good, that all we could do was just lay there in amazement.

"Damn, did that just happen?" I asked in amazement. "I was just about to ask you the same thing, I mean damn that was intense."
"Intense isn't a good comparison, damn, you need to be humbled of

yourself, Mr. Grant." "Ha, ha, what do you mean?" "You know exactly what I mean, you didn't tell me you were working with all this down here." Well, you didn't ask." "You got some good dick there, damn, my legs are still shaking, look can I just bottle all this up and keep it, ha, ha, I mean literally, you got some good, good, dick." I said in a whisper." "You're so funny, look who's holding back, you didn't tell me that you were carrying this wet pouch around." "Wet pouch, you mean my wet kitty, yes, she gets super wet but only for the right person, and damn did you make her wet and want you more, plus I have had sex in three years, so what do you expect?" "Hey baby, I am not complaining but there should be a crime walking around with all this good, good, ha, ha." "Ha, ha, boy, you're silly, but damn, Mr. Kenneth Grant, huh, can I keep you?" "Hell yeah, can I keep you?" "You are kept, baby," I said, and we started kissing and making love all over again. That was one of the best nights of my life.

The more we spent time together the more comfortable I felt around Kenneth and for the very first time, I felt safe. That's how he made me feel. I prayed night in and night out that this was for real and every time I woke up, I pinched myself to see if it was real.

All this time, I played it safe and kept my heart at bay, but I could no longer control it. Kenneth came into my life, and he swept me off my feet, who would have thought? "Damn, I think I am falling into the L-word, nope, nope, I can't say it yet, damn, is it true, I better take my ass to sleep, now, ha, ha," I said to myself as I got comfortable in my bed and fell asleep.

CHAPTER FOUR

My Body Want Sex But My Mind Wants Love

I must admit Kenneth had my head on cloud nine and my kitty on cloud ten. Hell, she jumped or started pulsating every time I got close to him. I knew right then he was the one and my girls must meet him.

I set up a date for them to all meet Kenneth at my house that following Saturday night, but first, I had to talk to them alone. I wanted to make sure they were not going to embarrass me for one. I could just think of all the times I said I didn't want a man and now I have one. At least he ain't an old ass man with dick problems, hell I bet I don't need a sugar daddy, plus I have pride and dignity, and I can buy my shit and pay my damn bills.

The girls and I met out at the Texas Brazil Restaurant. Everybody was all dressed up and ready to get some strong drinks in their system. I was feeling so good inside, and I couldn't wait to share all the good news with them about me and my new man.

"Hey, Hey, look at you, girl you're glowing," Marcella said. "Damn, you see it too, hmmm, somebody got some dick," Latisha said. "Oh my, damn, you're right, look, look, he got her ass walking funny too, look, right?" Giovanni said with a chuckle. "Will ya'll bitches be quiet up in here, you are talking too damn loud, I don't want these people in my fucking business," I said.

"Chill out, you need to calm down girl," Latisha said. "They can't hear us," Marcella whispered. "Stop, stop it, now let's order our drinks," I said. "Girl, we are going to order our drinks when the waitress comes but tell us about that man you're hiding," Latisha said. "I'm not hiding anyone, I just wanted to wait until the time was right until y'all meet him," I said. "Oh, so, now the time is right after he fucked you good?" Giovanni said. "Yeah, and got your ass opened," Marcella said. "Listen here, nobody got me open, see that's why I didn't want to tell ya'll shit, and if you keep it up, I won't," I said with an attitude.

"Oh, so, now little Miss I don't want a man to be all upset because we are clowning her little lying ass?" Latisha said. "Hey, can't a bitch change her mind?" I asked. They all stared me down and answered quickly, "No." "Damn, you guys are wrong," I said as I poked out my lips. "You better save those poked-out lips for that dick," Marcella said. "Shut up hoe, old nasty ass," I said. "Hey, I am, just saying," Marcella said. "You are funny as hell for that one, Marcella," Giovanni said. "Ha, ha, that's funny as fuck, pucker up baby, just suck it, just suck it," Latisha said as she started singing a nasty song.

"I knew I should've kept my mouth shut," I said angrily. "No. No, stop it, we are only messing with you, it's good to see you happy again and with a man." Marcella said. "Can't you take a joke, damn, is he a sugar daddy?" Giovanni asked. "No, we are around the same age," I said. "Well tell us about this knight in shiny armor," Marcella said. "I can't wait to meet him, are you going to keep this one?" Latisha asked. "The question is, is he going to keep me," I said. "You go ahead girl, you're the prize, right," Marcella said. "He knows it," I said. "I bet he does, he must have knocked those cobwebs off that stale pussy, ha, ha," Giovanni said, and they all started laughing, including me.

Shortly after our conversation, the waitress brought us our drinks. We talked, drank and we danced to some music. I talked about Kenneth most of the night. They were all eager to meet him and so was I.

"You know what, Loraine?" Giovanni said. "What, girl?" "You have that look of love in your eyes." She said. "You think so, am I that revealing," I asked. "Hell yeah, you're walking around here like you need some dick every second now," Latisha said. "Bitch, you are so stupid, but that shit is funny, ha, ha," Marcella said with a chuckle. "Will yall leave me alone, damn, okay, I fell for that man, shit, I am human," I said?

The girls made more jokes and I just started joking back about their sex lives. Eventually, we got off the joking and we started enjoying each other's company.

The next weekend came, the girls all met at my house, and I introduced them to Kenneth. All my girls just loved him. They told me how happy they were for me. It started getting late that evening and just as things were winding down, my doorbell rang. "Now, who the hell is this at my door?" I asked.

"Who is it?" "It's your mother, now let me in." "Mother, what are you doing here?" I asked her. I opened the door and hugged her. "Don't be hugging me now, get off me, now who's having a party?" She asked." "No one Mother, why are you here this late?" I asked. "Who is it, baby?" Kenneth said as he walked to the door. "Baby?" Mother said. "Oh, Kenneth this is my mother, mother this is Kenneth," I said with nervousness. "Hello, Mother." "Baby, huh, so you weren't lying about meeting a man?" Mother whispered. "No, I wasn't, Mother," I whispered back.

Mother walked on in the house and they all got acquainted with Kenneth. Marcella pulled out the cards and we started playing spades. I can tell they all like Kenneth and he likes them. I cannot believe it took me so many years to find the love of my life, especially when I wasn't even looking for it. That is, don't look for love, and let it find you. This is only the beginning, and I hope this is happy ever after, but only time will tell. As of now, I am truly in love with Kenneth Grant!

CHARLES LEE ROBINSON JR.

SOMETIMES,

A MAN JUST WANTS PEACE

PROLOGUE

TODAY:

You know, sometimes, all the man needs, or should I say all a man wants, is his peace. We work all day, most of us in a job that we don't like, but, we have to do it to make ends meet. It sounds easy, doesn't it? It's not, and on top of that, we, what should I say I, have to go home to my woman and deal with things in the household.

It's a lot on my shoulders, and you'll be surprised how strong I must be. My story, let me tell you a little something about it, I am Henry Freeman, but you can call me Hick.

After a bad breakup with my Ex, Valerie Henson, I decided that I would stay single and just talk or date whomever I wanted to. Things were going so well; I even got a new position as an Engineer.

For the very first time in a long time, I was at peace, and it felt so damn good. I mean not a care in the world; I was living drama-free.

It had taken me a while to build myself back up and feel like a man again. My Ex had brought so much bad energy into my life, that when she was no longer there, I started feeling like a brand-new man, with no goals, dreams, or aspirations.

You see, men often don't want to talk aloud because we love to think within ourselves and that's how we figure out things and the directions we want to take in our lives.

Peace of mind is a powerful thing, and that's why I loved being single for so long. The things Valerie put me through helped me to know that I had to be by myself to rebuild myself.

Now this isn't a bashing a woman's story, this is a true story and everyone has their side of the story, but I can only give you mine and I will let you be the judge.

CHARLES LEE ROBINSON JR.

CHAPTER ONE

Met Her At Marco J's

THE PAST:

"Hick, Mrs. Tavert wants to see you in the Human Resources department." My manager Kerry said. "For what?" I asked. "I guess some rumors have been going around." "What rumors, damn, I hate this shit," I said in a whisper. "I am not sure, just go talk to them," Kerry said as I walked off slowly.

After talking to the H.R. I was pissed. People on this job don't ever want to believe your word. It's always their word against mine. I went home very pissed and I immediately started looking for another job. That shit stressed me the hell out, but I tried not to let it get to me.

All I wanted was peace. I want to go to work do my job, make money that's it." It's always some bullshit with these jobs." I thought to myself.

The phone rang while I was looking online for employment. "Yo, Hick, what are you doing man." My friend Joey said. "Hey, my brother, I am just home, looking online for a new job." "A new job, what's wrong with that one?" "They are starting rumors, I mean lies, I think they just don't want me there." "Yeah, I understand that shit, I am going through it too, those people don't give a shit about you." "I know that's why I am looking now." Well, good luck on that, hey get your mind off that, and let's go out tonight and have a few drinks." "Whereabout, I am cool with that." "Let's hit Marco J's, I heard they have a lot of nice women there." "Oh, really, that might be a good idea, but I don't know about talking to a woman right now, man I am too damn stressed." "Maybe if you get your dick sucked you'll be all right, ha, ha." "Ha, ha, yeah right, that might get me into more problems." Hell knaw, man, that's the problem, you need some, you need a woman so you can get rid of all that stress, that's probably why your job getting on your nerves." "No, they are just assholes, but I don't know man, I don't want to meet anybody." "Man, are you fruity, come on, a good woman is what you need my brother." "Yeah right, I am about to get dressed, send me the address and I will meet you there in a couple of hours." "Okay bet, see you then, Hick."

At about 8 pm, I met Joey at Marco J's, and just like he said there were wall-to-wall women in there. We sat at the bar and we started ordering drinks, and then some hot wings.

When our food came, we decided to get a table and it happened to be next to a table full of beautiful women. They started staring at us and we drank and laughed out loud.

"You guys sound like y'all are having fun, can we join you?" A young lady said. "Sure, you can, hey, I am Joey and this is my friend Hick." "Nice to meet you Joey, and Hick, now I know your momma didn't name you, Hick, now did she?" "No, my name is Henry, but my friends and family call me Hick, and your name is?" "Oh, hey, I am Valerie and this is Tonya, Shamarra, Cynthia, and Marcella, it's a pleasure to meet you guys." She said.

Valerie and her friends came over to our table and the rest was history, We never laughed so hard that night. It was lots of fun. As we were leaving, Valerie and I exchanged numbers. "Call me tomorrow," Valerie said. "Okay, I will," I said. "See, I told you, you might meet someone nice, man, I like all of them, but I can only have one," Joey said. "Ha, ha, your horny, greedy ass, be careful, or your dick may fall off." "Hell no, don't wish that on me, but for thought, I think I like

Marcella the best." "No, you like her big breast, ass, and hips, ha, ha." "Yeah, I do, but they were all nice and sexy, but it's just something special about Marcella." "Did you get her number?" "Hell, yeah, right here." "Damn, you're fast and smooth." "Ha, ha, I wasn't letting all that ass go." "You know it's more to a woman than a big ass and tits, right?" "Sure, I know, but I don't want to find out." "Ha, ha, you are a fool." Ha, ha, you know I am, playing, but I see you and the old girl hitting it off." "With whom, Valerie, yeah I think she's hot." "I thought you didn't want a woman?" "Man, shut up," I said as we laughed our way out of Marco J's.

CHAPTER TWO

I Let Her Move in Too Fast

Valerie and I talked for several months and it seemed like everything was all good. I explained to her that I wanted to be in a serious and committed relationship, but I also needed peace.

Without peace in a relationship, we would have problems and I told her that. I explained my situation at work and how stressful it was and she seemed to understand.

I believe things changed when she lost her job and got evicted from her apartment. The landlord said she was late with her rent too many times. So, I decided to let Valerie live with me until she found a job and then an apartment.

She was so happy about those arrangements but I believe after a few months she started getting too comfortable. I would come home and dishes would be in the sink, I would ask her why she didn't clean them and she would say, "You live here, this is your house, you clean them." I couldn't believe that shit, it annoyed me especially when I was still going through all that crazy shit at work. Then she started leaving her weave all over the house and her wigs on the bathroom floor.

"Valerie, why is your wig on the floor and hair everywhere, I don't live like this, what's up?" "Oh, I just forgot, I am going to get them." She said.

My peace of mind was trampled. I got to the point where I didn't want to go straight home after work. I constantly asked her about her looking for a job, but it seemed like all she wanted to do was lay around my house all day.

I started having headaches because of the situation. I missed being home alone. It seemed like our relationship was better when we didn't live together.

Every day it was something different with Valerie. She would turn the air conditioner on low and I would be freezing. I asked her not to touch the thermostat and she just kept on doing it. At this point, I was hoping she would find a job quickly.

I was starting to feel disrespected in my own house. On top of that, I had a bad day, and the police pulled me over and gave me a $300 traffic ticket, when I came home to vent to her, she turned it around on me as if it was my fault. All I wanted her to do was listen, not condemn me.

Sometimes, all a man wants is an open ear, and it was getting frustrating talking to my woman and she only wanted to hear what she heard and not what I said.

CHARLES LEE ROBINSON JR.

Our communication started going out the window. I would pray to the Lord every day that she found a damn job.

I was only trying to help her but, now mentally, I needed help myself. I needed my peace badly, but I didn't want to hurt her feelings.

CHAPTER THREE

Taking My Kindness for Weakness

After two months, Valerie found a job. I was happy about that because I knew it wouldn't be long before she would find an apartment, at least I thought.

I came home one day and Valerie had her friends over. The house was a damn mess. It wasn't like that when I left for work that morning, so it pissed me off.

"Valerie, what are you doing, did you even go to work today?" "What does it look like, my girls came by so I decided to call in sick this morning, why are you bugging me?"

It took everything in me to not show my ass in front of her friends. I shook my head and I went upstairs to shower, I could hear them talking loudly and blasting music. I didn't even go back downstairs, I just laid across my bed because I was so exhausted from my day at work.

Valerie and her friends didn't let up until a little after midnight and I had to work in the morning. She came to bed at almost 1 am and to top it all off she thought she could ease in my bed and give me head and think that I would forget all about it. I did accept the blow job but right after, I went to sleep while she was still trying to spark a conversation with me.

The next morning, we argued about what happened. "You have to find your place," I said. "So, now you want me to leave when you know, I can't provide for myself now?" "You can't provide for yourself, aren't you a grown-ass woman?"

"That's nasty to say, I can't believe this shit, if you felt that way why didn't you stop me from sucking your duck last night?" I immediately got quiet and then I paused before saying something to her.

"You think sucking my dick is going to fix all this, before you were living here, I had peace, I miss that, ever since you have been here it's been chaos and turmoil, don't you as a grown-ass woman think it's time for you to get your own, I mean you do, still, have your job right?"

"Yes, I do, I will find a place and get out of your hair since you don't want me." She said. "I never said I didn't want you, but as my woman, you should understand how I feel, I told you from the beginning that you can't come into my life if you weren't going to bring me peace."

"Fine, I will look for a place when I get off work today, I have to get ready for work, I am going to be late because of you, I can't believe how you are treating me." "How am I treating you, I let you come to my home as if it was yours, and we had an agreement that you would find a job and then get you a place."

"Whatever, I will get out of your damn house, fine," Valerie said as she started grabbing her clothes and ran into the bathroom, and slammed the door off the hinges.

I was truly pissed now because she was not cleaning shit and now she's tearing up shit. I wanted her ass out of my house asap.

CHAPTER FOUR

The Communication Part

One day after work, I decided to go over to Joey's house because I didn't even want to go home. Valerie was still there and hadn't found an apartment yet. All we did was argue, so I decided to go talk to my boys.

"Hey guys, look who's here, it's lover boy, Hick." My friend Teddy said. "Hey boy, come on in here," Mike said. "Hey what's up fellas, you didn't tell me these fools were in here, Joey." "They just got here actually, they just decided to drop by."

"Okay, so what's up fellas, and stop calling me lover boy, y'all know I hate that shit, I only talk to one woman and one woman only," I said. "Yeah, he's in love now," Joey said as he laughed.

"Who is she, who's the lucky lady?" Teddy asked. "Her name is Valerie," I said. "I heard you already moved her into your house, damn she must have sucked your little dick really good," Mike said and they all started laughing.

"Damn, Joey, are you telling my business?" I asked as I turned to Joey. His face turned red and he said, "Come on man, we all fellas, right, the guys were just asking what was going on with their boy, so I told them." "Talkative ass men, I tell you," I said. "Come on man, calm down, it ain't nothing, everything is all right, right?" Teddy asked. "It's not all that good, I can't lie," I said. "Damn, I am sorry to hear that," Mike said. "Why didn't you tell me?" Joey asked. "Man, I was trying to work things out," I said.

I told the guys everything that was going on and after that, we just started talking about women and relationships.

"Sorry to hear what you're going through; did you guys even communicate with each other before she moved in?" Mike asked. "We communicated all the time when we first met, but now, all we do is argue," I said.

"Man, I hate that shit, why don't women understand that all we want is peace, I am sure you told her over and over again," Joey said. "Man, women don't care if we have peace or not, they always say that we don't communicate, I think they just over-communicate," Teddy said.

"What the hell is an over-communicate?" Mike asked. "You know what it is," Joey said. "I'm starting to think you don't even know what it is," Teddy said. "I think I have an idea what he's trying to say, but, Joey, please explain," I said.

"What I am trying to say is that women want us to be able to communicate like them, they want us to express more, talk more, you know, just like them," Joey said.

"I can agree with that, but I am always attentive to my woman and I always say from the beginning how I want things and how I want our relationship," I said.

"Well, apparently she didn't get the memo," Mike said. "Apparently not," I said. "So, what are you going to do?" Joey asked. "I asked her to move out," I said. "This joker is cold, boy, you said what?" Mike asked. "I told her I want her out," I said. "What did she say?" Teddy asked. "She said she was going to move out," I said. "And, you believe her?" Joey asked. "Why not?" I asked.

"You better be careful because these women don't like rejection, you mess around and your whole house be burned down," Teddy said. "You remember that girl, Tisha, I used to talk to, that damn girl stole out of my house and all my underwear was torn up," Mike said. "Yeah, I remember that she was crazy as hell," Joey said with laughter. "Yeah, Hick, you better be careful because women like that don't like rejection and they don't like to be told what to do," Teddy said. "I am not worried, Valarie isn't like that," I said. "Are you sure?" They all answered at the same time.

"Listen, on a serious note, if you both communicated at the beginning, then she should know better, she should know that she's violating your peace." Mike said, "That's right, men love their peace too, if I was you, I would kick her ass to the curb asap." Teddy said.

"Y'all going to make Hick get his ass kicked when he gets home," Joey said and they all laughed. "Right, well let me get home, I have to let her know," I said. "You do that," Mike said. "Later man," Joey said as I walked out of the door.

CHAPTER FIVE

A Man Just Wants His Peace

I made it home and as soon as I walked into my house, Valerie was lying around and the house was a mess. I walked into the bathroom and her weave was all in the tub and on the bathroom floor.

"Valerie, can you please clean your hair up in the bathroom?" I asked and she just ignored me.

"Did you hear me?" "Yes, I heard you, can't you see I am watching TV?" "First of all, this is my house, and I deserve respect." "Old, Mr. Arrogant ass." "How in the hell is that acting arrogant, never mind, don't answer that, have you found a place yet?" "Does it look like it?" "You know what, get your things and leave now." "I ain't going anywhere, at least until I feel like it, and you can't make me do shit, it's the law." "The law my ass, I want you out of my house, I've had it with your slack living ass, I don't live like this and I have peace in my house, but you have somehow, taken that peace away from here and I want you out." "Like I said, I ain't going no, damn, where." "You're not, huh?" I said and Valerie ignored me.

That shit pissed me off. Here I was thinking I was doing something nice by helping her out and she ended up being an evil demon.

"Will you please leave; I don't want you here." "Fine, I am going, I need to get the fuck out of this man's house." She said as she got up and started slamming my doors.

"Hey, hey, stop slamming my fucking doors." "You don't tell me what to do, you want me out of here, I am getting out of here." She said as she started throwing her clothes on the floor.

All I could do was put my hands up in the air. I was trying to help this girl and now she was disrespecting me and my home, It was so quiet and peaceful in my home before she came.

I watched her walk around in circles, just talking shit to me but not grabbing any of her things, so I started putting her things in bags. "Don't touch my shit, I didn't ask you for any help." She yelled. "Girl, just go." "What does it look like I am doing?" She yelled.

"Truthfully, I can't tell because you're not moving fast enough." "You don't rush me, if you keep talking, I will burn all this shit down." "Hey, hey, don't threaten me like that, I want you gone now, for real, get your shit and get the hell out." "Fuck you and your house, I don't need you."

As soon as Valerie said that, I started putting her things in big bags and putting them out on the porch. "Hey, what are you doing, no one told you to touch my things." "As long as they are in my house I am touching them so, uhm, hello, goodbye, get your shit."

"You are a dirt, mean man, I can't believe you are kicking me out, I don't have anywhere to go." "That's not my problem, I am sure you have someplace to go or somewhere to stay, that's not my problem." "You know what Hick, you are an ass, I don't need this shit, I am gone." She said as she stumbled out the door with a bag with some of her things in it." "Good riddance," I said loudly. "Fuck you," Valerie yelled.

Just as I thought she was gone I heard the air from my tires on my car pop and a loud window crashing sound. I looked out the door and

Valerie started bashing the windows out of my car and stabbing my tires one by one.

I ran outside and she started running away while leaving her bags of clothes. "Fuck you, you are going to get yours, Hick, I promise you that, you arrogant asshole." She screamed.

Several of my neighbors came outside to see what all the commotion was about and I never felt so embarrassed in my life. All these years I had been living a peaceful life and as soon as I let my guard down, I got all this chaos, but never again.

When it was all said and done, Valerie had to pay for all the damages she caused or the other option was that I press charges. Sometimes, men just want someone they can talk to and relate to.

I just wanted peace and I was trying to help her, but some people, you just can't help and I will never jeopardize the peace in my home ever.

The End!!!

CHARLES LEE ROBINSON JR.

JUST TO SAY I GOT A MAN

CHAPTER ONE

I Won't Settle

Once again, I woke up horny as hell, here I am all alone, again. I have a master's degree, I'm independent, and pretty, and still can't seem to find a good man. Night after night I have to please myself and my toys are getting played out.

I went to work stressed that morning, thinking about being lonely and living alone. I ain't going to lie, I don't want to seem thirsty for a man because I will not settle. As soon as I made it to the hospital, I ran into my colleague, Rochelle. "Hey April, what's new, and why are you looking sad?" "I am not sad, maybe horny as hell," I said, and we both laughed.

Rochelle is cool as hell but the only thing I don't like is she has a sorry-ass man at home, he doesn't work, cook, or clean, apparently, all he does is give her some dick. Time after time I try to tell her to leave that sorry-ass man, but she just won't, that man probably got some good dick, that's why she probably doesn't want to let his sorry-ass go.

Besides that, Rochelle is still one of my closest friends, and then there is Amanda. She's pretty cool too, but she's another one who has a man, well half a fucking man because he's always putting his hands on her, and sometimes, she comes to work with black eyes. I swear I would hang that asshole by his dick and nuts if he ever puts his hands on me, plus I've been through that shit before, and I promised myself that will never happen to me ever again. I don't know what's wrong with these women, but they better wake the hell up.

At the same time, you must ask yourself who raised these men that they would put their hands on a woman or treat a woman like shit? Who? Huh?

Then last but not least is my friend Sylvia. This whore is a trip. She loves women but she's only with a man because she wants to stay on the down low. The man is skinny, dark as charcoal with big ass teeth, but maybe I am exaggerating a bit, but he's funny looking, but he's nice.

"Hey Silvia, are you still with that skinny man?" "Yeah, we are still an item." "Yeah, right, are you still seeing that chick Armenia?" "Oh, we're just friends." "Stop that damn lying girl, I saw you two kissing behind the movie theater last week, y'all aren't slick," I said. "Look, April, it isn't what you think, we are just friends," Silvia said. "Yeah, y'all are just friends who put their tongues in each other's mouths," I said. "Shh, shh, keep it down." She said. "Girl, all I can say is, you are confused, and your friend is too, you mean to tell me you will do all this just to say you got a man, are you out of your mind? "I said in a whisper.

The girls and I, while at work, just talked about wack-ass men all day. We barely got anything done, but when the clock struck five, I was on my way home.

Once again, I was in this big ass house all alone, with nothing to do. I sat down on my sofa, and I started to call my momma, but I knew she would talk a lot of shit to me about being in this big ass house alone.

I sat there shaking my leg and then I turned on the news. There wasn't anything on TV worth watching, all they showed was black men killing black men. I jumped up and I went into my room. I took off all my clothes and I went into my bathroom.

It had been a long day and it was now time to unwind. I usually take hot showers but tonight I decided to put my fine ass in the tub. I ran the water exactly right and then I put some pretty-smelling bubble bath in the tub. I put some candles around the tub and then I went into the kitchen to get a bottle of wine and a glass. I hurried back into the bathroom before the water in my tub overflowed, and I plopped my fine, and tired ass, right in the water. It was so damn soothing, oooweee.

After almost falling asleep in the tub, I got out and grabbed my towel and I walked into my bedroom still a little wet. I started drying myself off slowly and I started daydreaming as if a man was touching me and caressing me.

At that point, there wasn't anything else to do but scratch the itch that I was having. My hot box was steaming hot, and I wanted so badly to make love to a strong man. So, I knew I had to please myself because there was no way I was going to settle. I lay in my bed with my legs open wide and started taking care of myself in the only way I knew how. I brought out my sexual toys and I took a little edge off. When it was all said and done, I was feeling so good. I got up and showered again, grabbed my pillow, put it between my thick legs, and rocked from side to side.

Yes, of course, I felt the want of a man, but there's no way in hell am I to give just any man a chance to fuck me good, but he doesn't care about me, or he doesn't have any substance to him. That's the shit I used to do in the past, but I am a grown-ass woman now. That's why I can't understand why my friends are going through this toxic cycle with these no-good, sorry-ass, men.

Just as I was thinking about what I wanted and what I needed, I got a disturbing phone call. "Hey April, it's Ms. Brooks, Amanda's mother, jumped on my baby and now she's in the hospital, I know you're one of Amanda's friends, can you come to the hospital now?" Ms. Brooks said, and I could hear her break down and cry. "Yes, I will be right there," I said as I was in utter disbelief.

I told that girl for years now to leave that sorry muthafucka alone, now look, he put her ass in the hospital. I promptly called Silvia and Rochelle and they both said they would meet me at the hospital. I was furious with her but also scared because I was hoping he hadn't put her on her deathbed.

When we made it there, both of Amanda's eyes were swollen and so was her jaw. We were all in tears. "I am so sorry Ms. Brooks," I said. "Oh, hey, look what he did to my baby." She said as she put her nose in her tissue and started crying more. "Are you okay, how is she?" I asked. "He needs his ass kicked by a man as he did her," Rochelle said. Amanda whispered that she was okay. "I can't wait until I get my hands on him," I said. "Do any of you ladies, know where this man is?" Ms. Brooks asked. "No, I don't," I said and so did the girls. We were all clueless, but we vowed to whoop his ass when we see his ass. After a day or so, they let Amanda out of the hospital. Her wounds took a while to heal but after a month or so, she was back to normal.

Although that sorry-ass man put her in the hospital, she refused to press charges against him. I was fearful that she would take him back, again, just to say she had a man like she couldn't get another one.

I wanted to put a stop to that notion, so I invited all the girls over to my house for drinks and to just talk about some things. I wanted to open up their eyes to the things I went through when I was with a narcissist and toxic ass man.

"Hey ladies, I invited you gals here because, what happened to Amanda, should've never happened, and I hope to open you lady's eyes today, you are a beautiful woman and you should know your worth, I don't know what I would do if I lost either one of you," I said. "Thank you, girls, for being there for me," Amanda said with half of a smile.

"You know we love you girl, and you gave us a scare," Sylvia said. "Have you spoken to that man since then?" Rochelle asked and Amanda got quiet. "Girl no, tell me you are not thinking about getting back with that monster?" Silvia said. "No, no, but he has been begging me back, I haven't given him an answer," Amanda said. "Girl, you are a glutton for punishment," Rochelle said. "Listen, ignore his ass, he almost killed you, that's why I invited you, ladies, here so you don't make the same mistakes I did in the past, and that's why I don't give a toxic man a chance to come into my life, I am strong now, so with that being said, I want to tell you guys about how I escaped a bad relationship with a lazy, sorry, mean, jealous, asshole," I said and all the ladies got comfortable as I began to tell my story.

CHAPTER TWO
He Treated Me Like Shit

I still remember it like it was yesterday. At the time I was insecure because I'd always been an overweight woman. I worked a lot, and I was a homebody, I didn't want anyone I knew to see me fat like that. I was lonely and I just wanted someone to love me.

Then came Victor Squire, we worked together at the nursing home on South Avenue, in Rochester, New York. He was so nice to me, and he said he didn't care that I was four hundred pounds. He called me pretty all the time and that made me blush. Victor was a handsome man, and I would always ask him why he liked a woman like me, as good as he looked, and he would always say, stop saying that about yourself. I would smile and blush. I was too naïve to realize he was just sweet-talking me to get into my panties and take my money. His words made me feel good and wanted, so I fell into his trap.

It took me a while before I slept with him but when I did that was when everything changed. While I was falling deeply in love with him, he was only playing games with my heart, now what kind of man would do something like that? I am not going to lie, he laid it down on me in the bedroom and I guess that's one of the reasons, fell for him so easily. But a few weeks after we slept together, he started changing.

CHARLES LEE ROBINSON JR.

"Where the hell have you been with your fat ass?" "What, what do you mean, I just came from work?" "Oh yeah, who are you fucking at work, with your fat ass?" "I don't know why you keep calling me fat, you weren't saying that when you were all up inside me?" I said.

"Shut the hell up, next time, tell me where you are at." "That's stupid, you know I am a homebody, so I'm either home or at work." "Don't you talk back to me," "I am not talking back, Victor I am grown okay, and I have feelings," "I don't give a shit about your feelings," He said and I just sat there and cried. I was so confused because the man I fell in love with wasn't this man, right here. I don't know who the hell was this man, I guess he gave me his representative at first. I dealt with his mental abuse every day, and I didn't want to let him go because all my friends had a man, and I didn't want to be alone.

He would talk badly about me in front of his friends and sometimes in front of his family. His sister Thelma and I became great friends, and he didn't like that shit. Behind his back, Thelma would say, "You are too good for my brother, you should leave his ass." I listened to her, but my insecurities wouldn't let me walk away from him.

The more he talked about me the more I fed my face with food. One day I had a slight heart attack. I was in the hospital for almost a week and Victor never came to the hospital to see me. As soon as I got out of the hospital, he all of a sudden magically appeared. The doctor said I needed to lose weight, but I couldn't explain that the stress from my relationship was causing me to eat.

"Why didn't you come to see me while I was in the hospital?" "I was going to come, but I was out looking for a job." What do you mean you were out looking for a job, what happened to the job at the nursing home?" "Man, I quit that shit, they were talking to me fucked up, so I walked out." You walked out, you can't just walk out of a job when you feel like it." The hell I can't." So, what are you going to do for money and the bills?" "Nothing, you will pay all that." "What do you mean I will pay all that, I just got out of the hospital, and I have to wait two weeks for my disability check to come." "So, what, you have money, you can pay all the bills, I will get a job soon," Victor said.

A few weeks after I was released from the hospital, my mother came by to see me. "I see you are looking better, how are you feeling?" "I am okay, Mom." "Are you sure, you look stressed, now you know I can feel that something isn't right, a mother knows her children, right?" "Well, truthfully, I am stressed out." "Why because of that man?" "Yes, Lord, he quit his job, Mom." "He did what, I hate to be the one to tell you, but you better talk with him." "Mom, I did, and he still hasn't found a job." "April, I am your Mom and you know I hate to get in your and your sister, Monique's business, but I have to say this if a man isn't treating you right, get rid of his ass, I went through shit like this with your Dad many years ago." "I know you told me the story." "Then you better listen and what was his excuse about not coming to see you in the hospital?" "He didn't have any." "Get rid of his sorry ass, you are a beautiful woman and I raised you to have a beautiful heart, he's not worth it, and I hate to see you in the hospital again." "I know Mom, I will handle it," I said. "Handle what?" Victor said as he crept into the house. "Oh nothing, okay Mom, I will talk to you later," I said. "You remember what I said," Mom said as she grabbed her coat to leave. "Goodbye, Ma'am," Victor said, and Mom just ignored him. "What's wrong with her?" He asked, "Nothing, where have you been?" "None of your business, where is my food, did you cook it, did you eat it with your fat ass?" "I wish I would cook you something, cook it yourself." "Who are you talking to?" "The fridge and stove are that way," I said as I pointed toward the kitchen.

"Damn, you are lazy, I should've never started talking to you, look at you, you are sloppy looking, all out of shape, that's okay I will cook something myself." "Now, I am sloppy looking, I can't believe you are talking to me that way and hurting my feelings." "Shut up, lose some damn weight, you weren't that big when I met you." "No, I wasn't but you are the one who's making me gain all this weight." "Don't blame me, you already were thick but now, damn, if you keep it up, no man will want your fat ass." He said. I ran upstairs, I jumped on my bed, and I cried. He didn't care that he was hurting me. After that, I started getting sick and I was in and out of the hospital every week or so. Victor didn't care, he just kept doing him.

The doctor urged me to start exercising and to eat healthily but every time Victor was around, he stressed me the hell out, so I ate, and I ate, and the weight kept piling up. I would look in the mirror and I didn't like what I saw. My coke bottle shape was gone, and I felt just like Victor said, that no man would ever want me.

Victor made me feel like the lowest of the low and all the while, I was still taking care of him and making sure he had some money, food, and a place to stay. I was a fool and my mom constantly told me to leave his ass where I found him. It got to the point that even my elder sister told me to move on and she said, "You don't need that lazy ass man, sis, you are too good for him." I heard them loud and clear, but I didn't want to be alone, I wanted to have a man just like everybody else.

Sometimes, when I was sick, he would take my car and would be gone for hours not knowing if I needed to go anywhere or not. He stole money from my purse and then he would deny it. I felt helpless in my own home, it was like he didn't care if I lived or died.

The way Victor changed on me and as fast as he did, I knew that couldn't have been love. I loved him with all my heart, and he was taking advantage of me, but I was too scared to let my man go, even if he was only half a man.

CHAPTER THREE

He Was Cheating

No matter what Victor did, I stayed in the relationship with hopes that one-day things would change back to the way things were when I first met him, but that was only wishful thinking.

Victor was constantly cheating me and to make it so bad, I knew, but I didn't do a damn thing about it, because I was too scared. I thought that as soon as I made him leave, he would be with someone else and I would be all alone, how stupid did that sound?

His clothes always smelled like a woman's perfume, and he always came in and ran his cheating ass right into the shower. I could've sworn one night, I smelled a woman's pussy on him, and if I did, I knew she was a dirty whore.

Of course, he would deny and lie about it, but deep down, I knew. Just like a stupid ass chick, I would let him sweet talk me in some way. "I am not cheating on you, that's all in your mind." He would say. I would give him a dirty look and I would say, "Okay, then why do you smell like a woman's perfume?" "Maybe some chick rubbed up against me, hell, I don't know." Now, how in the hell you don't know if somebody rubbed up against you and they are smelling good? Victor definitely thought I was a damn dummy. I took the mental abuse repeatedly and it was wearing me down. It's a crazy thing, it seemed the more he downed me and said evil things to me, the more I loved him, at least that's how my tormented mind felt. How could I love a man, who I knew didn't love me?

I tried to fall out of love with him, but I couldn't. I was trapped in a fantasy world, and I couldn't let go, even if I wanted to. They say if a person shows who they really are, believe them, but I just couldn't get myself to believe that I was meant to be alone.

My Mom would constantly tell me being alone wasn't a terrible thing. I would ignore her because even she had a man. I was getting all kinds of abuse from Victor and my morale started going down. I felt down all the time and my energy was low. I was dipping down into depression and when I rolled over in my bed at night, my man wasn't there. I knew he was out in the streets fucking some bitch, but I refused to cut ties with him and move on.

I was destroying myself and my boundaries were only an illusion. Being the loving woman I was, I just took all his shit and I prayed from day to day and night to night. Every morning I got up, I was hoping I was waking up from this nightmare that I was living in. Although I was able to leave my house when I wanted to, I felt like a prisoner in my home.

After being out of work for nearly a month, I went back. As I walked down the halls at work, I heard all kinds of chatter and gossip. As I was leaving my shift, my co-worker Jo-Ann walked up to me and whispered, "Hey, did you know Julia and Victor were seeing each other when he was working here?" "What, no, I didn't, Victor never said a thing," "Well I am not here to start anything but from what Joann was saying, they are still fuck one another." "Who said that that has to be a damn lie," I said out of anger. "Keep it down, I am just telling you what I heard, and I felt that you should know." "Thank you but no thanks," I said as I ran out of the building.

I jumped into my car, and I drove around in my car. I finally stopped right in front of the house, and I just cried. "Why, why Lord, why would he do this to me, I loved him with all my heart, why would he cheat on me and why would he make a fool of me like that?"

I sat in my car for nearly an hour just crying and praying. My ears and my prayers were interrupted by a knock on my car window. I looked up and my sister Monique was standing there with her hands on her hips, with a mean-ass look on her face.

"Baby Sis, what are you doing, girl are you crying, get your ass out of this car now, and why aren't you in the house?" "Huh, oh, I didn't see you there," I said as I cracked the car's window. "Yeah, I know, now get out, and what's wrong with you, I talked to Mom and I told her I would check on you." "Check on me for what, I am okay." I said as I tried to hide and wipe the tears off my face, "Don't wipe those tears now, I see you, where is that man?" "I don't know," I said as I slowly got out of my car. I know you're not crying over his ass because if you are, that's going to stop today." "No, no, that's not the reason, I was just praying." "And that made you cry, come on now, Sis, I know better than that, are you still letting this man treat you like shit, now you know Mom and Big Mom taught us better than that." "I am okay, I'm okay, it's nothing." "Listen, I don't know who you think you are fooling, but I know you and I see right through you," Monique said as we walked into my house.

"Now when are you going to wake up and walk out, he'll this is your house, just kick his ass out," she said. I immediately started crying and my sister grabbed me in her arms, and she started hugging me.

"You don't deserve this, Sis, leave his ass alone." I know I know; I am so good to that man, and he treats me like shit, what did I do to deserve this?" "Nothing, Sis, absolutely nothing, he's just an asshole, you just have to find it in yourself to let him go, cut your ties, hell, yall don't have kids together." She said.

We talked for hours and hours and finally, she left after I was finished crying. About three hours later, Victor came home, and he smelled like he had been drinking all night. He showered and then he jumped into bed. I wanted to say something to him about what I heard at work, but I knew it would be a big argument because he was too intoxicated. So, I let him sleep until morning. When morning came, I woke up with an attitude. "So, what's up with you, what's up with us, are you cheating on me or what?" I said as I crossed my arms. "What, what the hell are you talking about, now?" "You heard me, are you cheating on me?" "What the hell are you talking about, I am drunk still, can't you see?" "Victor stops being funny, you know what I am saying, now answer the damn question, are you sleeping with other women?" "Yeah, I am, now what?" "You are what?" "Hey, I just told you what you wanted to hear." "Stop playing gamed Victor and why you didn't tell me that you were fucking Julia?"

"Julia, who is that?" "Now, you are playing stupid, you better not be, that's all I know." "Even if I was what are you going to do about it, you ain't going anywhere." He said with a lot of confidence. "Okay, keep playing these games, one day you will see." "Whatever, you are not going to do anything, and I am not going anywhere." He said and he slammed the bathroom door in my face as I walked behind him.

That shit burned me up inside, but it was true to what he said, I wasn't going to do a damn thing about it. How could I be so gullible? After I let that one slide more girls were popping up saying that they were sleeping with Victor. I would get text messages on my phone, and emails, and one bitch had the nerve to walk up to my front door and ask for Victor. I guarantee this, I bet that heffa won't do that again.

I gave him so many chances and I just looked like a damn fool every time. He would just walk around the house like he was the boss, and he wasn't doing a damn thing as far as a job.

He truly hurt me when I found out he was fucking another girl at my job named, Rachael. He and I worked on the same floor, and we constantly interacted with each other with the patients, and not one time did she elude anything to me about Victor. That bitch smiled in my face and all the time she was sleeping with my man.

I only found out by mistake because she talks too damn much. I overheard her saying some nasty shit about me and talking about how she's fucking my man. I was shocked when I heard her. A part of me wanted to kick her fucking ass, but I wanted to keep my job, I just ran into one of the offices and I cried, and I cried.

A few weeks after that, Rachael was fired. I was not behind her firing, but I was glad she was gone. It was so hard working with her every day, especially when I knew she was sleeping with Victor.

He and I got into so many arguments about it. He would always lie and make excuses by bringing my weight into it, but I knew what he was doing, he was being a manipulator and a liar. Even after all that, I didn't make him leave. I just kept being a loving woman and dealing with all of his lies. The thought of me being alone terrified me, so I kept my mouth shut for a while. How stupid was I?

CHAPTER FOUR

He Started Fighting Me

I guess after all the lying and cheating Victor was doing, I was getting fed up with him. I was always irritated when he was around. I couldn't be at peace in my own home. Our talks always became huge arguments, and I was sick in tired of being sick and tired.

He just came into the house and commanded orders. Now, why would I cook for a man who doesn't respect me? "I see you haven't cooked shit?" "I see you haven't bought anything for me too, cook," I said. "Keep getting smart with me." "Man, please, I am not cooking for a man that thinks his shit doesn't stink and won't even come into my house at a decent hour." "What did you say with your fat ass?" "You heard me, Victor, I am not scared of you, you heard what I said." "Keep talking, that's all I have to say." I ignored him and I kept cleaning up the house. Far as I was concerned, his ass could starve.

Almost every other day, we got into it, and he would always threaten to put his hand on me. I knew at the time; that I should shut my mouth and walk away.

For months we just couldn't get along, and I was exhausted. I needed someone to talk to, so I decided to call my Dad. He lived in California and he and I hadn't talked in a while. I guess I felt like he was the only person I could talk to about my situation without being judged about it.

"Hey, hey, April, I was just thinking about you." "You were, then why didn't you call me?" "Actually, I was just about to, I talked to your mother and your sister, and they told me what was going on with you." "They did, dang, they talk too much, I wanted to be the one to tell you." "Don't get mad at them for caring about you, so what's going on, are you okay, I heard you were in and out of the hospital too, I am upset about that because nobody called me." "I was I am sorry Dad; it's just been hectic in my life." "I understand that we all have problems, but you are still my baby girl and I think that I should know these things." "You're right, you're right, I am sorry Dad." "No need for apologies, so tell me what's going on with this Victor guy, you're dating or seeing," I told Dad everything that was going on and he kept encouraging me and telling me that I would do better. I couldn't help but start crying while I was on the phone with him.

"April, stop that crying, look you're a grown-ass woman now and I can't tell you how to run your life but I've taught you to be stronger than that, so first off, I want you to get into the gum, take kickboxing, yoga or whatever you need to do so you can stay healthy as your doctor said and while you are getting yourself on track you need to let that man know if he's not there to be with you, then his ass has to go." Okay, I will Dad." "Are you scared of him, does he hit you?" "No, I am not scared of him. He hasn't hit me, but I just don't want to be alone." "Baby girl stop that bullshit, you came into this world alone, well, I mean your Mom and I was there, but you don't have a twin, so that means you came into this world alone." "Ha, ha, Dad you have a weird way of putting things but that was funny, thank you for making, me. smile." "You know what I am, trying to say, let him know how you feel and if he puts his hands on you, call me, I will take the first flight out, and see what he will do to a real man, your father." "No, Dad, I will talk to him, don't you worry," I said. We talked for a little while longer and then I hung up the phone.

As soon as I hung up the phone, Victor walked in, and he was drunk and angry. "Who the hell were you on the phone with?" "None of your business, you don't pay this phone bill." I am going to ask you one more time, who the hell were you on the phone with?" "Nine of your damn business, that's who," I said as I started to walk away. "Don't you fucking walk away from me, I know you were on the phone with a damn man, I heard a man's voice." "Were you listening to my conversation, were you being sneaky and shit?" "This is the last time, I am, going to ask you, who are you fucking, was that a man on the phone?" "Who am I fucking, I should be asking you that with all those stank whores you've been talking to; I don't have to tell you anything, you're not my Dad." "I don't have to be your Dad, as matter of a fact, fuck your Dad." He said and I turned my back on him to walk away, I felt a blow to the back of my head, and I fell. My head hit the corner of the coffee table and I caught myself with my left hand on the sofa.

Victor jumped on top of me before I could get up and he punched me in my face several times. I was trying to get up, but the extra weight was holding me down. I started screaming for help, but no one came, and no one heard a thing. "Get off of me, stop, stop, why are you hitting me and punching me like a man?" "I told you don't play with your smart-ass mouth, now what man are you fucking, so I can whoop his ass too." He said as he whopped me in my eye, and my eyes started to swell instantly. "Ah, ah, stop, why are you hitting me, you going to pay for this." "What bitch?" He said and he hit me again. I tried to fight him, but he was too strong.

He didn't stop beating on me until he was tired. My body and my face were sore. He left out the house mad. I felt like a piece of shit, and I was embarrassed. At that moment, I wanted him out of my house. I started getting his things together and throwing all his shit in a big pile. I sat near all his shit with a big butcher knife in my hand. I called my sister Monique, and I told her what had happened. She wanted to come over to help me, but I told her to stay out of it. "If you don't want me to come to kick his ass, at least, call the police." She said. "I will, I will handle it, please don't tell Mom or Dad," I said. Monique promised me and she hung up the phone quickly.

For a whole week Victor didn't come home but every night I slept by his clothes and other shit with my big ass butcher knife. Finally, he returned with his, "I'm sorry, can you please let me in, I won't hit you again." My mind told me to don't do it, but my heart believed him and just wanted to give him one more chance.

How could I let this man in after what he did to me? My mind was working in overdrive. I was heartbroken and yet, I still felt alone. Victor begged and he begged and like a foolish little bitch, I gave in. Within a week, he was back to calling me every name under the sun. Right after I slept with his ass, he started showing his ass. "You sloppy fat bitch, I told you no man would want you, that's why you were still alone." "Victor, why are you hurting me this way, I thought you said it was going to be different this time, and now I look like a damn fool for letting you back in my house and letting you back in my life." "What life, you don't have a life." He said. When he said that, I felt his words cut through my soul like a knife.

The night he left the house, I grabbed all of his shit once again and put it near the door for him to get. I put my butcher knife under the sofa just in case he tried to hit me again. Victor came in and he immediately started complaining about me not cooking his disrespectful ass no food.

"I am not cooking you anything, especially after all the names you called me." "What the hell did you say?" "You heard me, now leave, I want you out of my house." "What, what are my clothes and things doing here, on the floor?" "That's your shit and I want you out." "I am not going anywhere, old fat sloppy ass better shut up and go to bed." "Victor, go, go, get out of my house," I screamed.

"What, I am not going anywhere, now put all my shit back, now." He yelled. "I said get out, get out," I said as I nudged him. Before I could say another word, he slapped me so damn hard, I felt like my brain was coming through my ear and my ear felt like it rang like a telephone for at least five minutes.

"Ahhh, you hit me, ahhh." I screamed as tears started falling down my cheeks. I started swinging and punching as I fought his ass back. He started kicking and punching and dragging me all over the house. I tried to get to my butcher knife as he sat on top of me and punched me in my head several times. I almost got my hand on the tip of my knife, but I couldn't grab it because he was hitting me so hard. I must have passed out from one of his blows because when I came to, I heard a commotion. As I looked up, I could see two men fighting and tussling and then I heard my sister Monique's mouth. "Get him, Daddy." She was yelling. By the time I came all the way conscience, I could see my Dad and Victor fighting.

"Are you okay Sis, get his ass Da, hold up let me get a lick," Monique said. "That's right Dad, I want him out of my house," I screamed. My Dad started kicking Victor's ass, and his clothes were torn off his body. Dad, drug Victor out of the house all beaten up, and then Monique and I shot all his shit out in the streets.

My head was pounding with a headache and my lip was big, bloody, and busted, and I was in tears. "Stop crying," Dad said. "How did y'all know what was going on?" I asked. "I told your neighbor if she hears anything that even sounds like two people fighting to let me know," Monique said. "And, you called Dad?" "I called Dad three days ago and he said he was coming here." "He won't be coming back here for a while, he has the damn nerve to put his hands on my daughter, I swear I will kill that muthafucka." "Dad, please don't do that, I don't want you to go to jail." "Fuck jail, no man has the right to hit a woman, especially not one of my daughters." "You flew from California?" "I sure did, I told you I would, and I didn't tell you because I knew you would try to talk me into staying here, but your sister Monique called me and told me what he did to you weeks ago." "She did, now, did she, I thought I told you not to tell Mom and Dad?" I whispered. "I didn't tell Mom, but I had to tell Dad." She said as she held up her fist. "Damn, Dad, I wouldn't want to be your enemy, you kicked his ass all over this house," Monique said. "He sure did, I woke up and I didn't know what was going on," I said. "I blacked out once I walked in and I saw you unconscious." He said as he started punching his hand in his other hand.

"I didn't know what was going on, I was out of it, but did y'all get in?" I asked. "That stupid fool left the door open." He said. "Listen, April whatever you do, don't let that man back up in here, get you a gun, or go start boxing and working out in the gym, or something, you need to be able to protect yourself, you are a beautiful woman and you don't deserve what that punk was trying to do to you, do you hear me?" "Yes, Dad, I know, I will get myself back." "You better, because if he comes back, the next time, I am going to kill him," Dad said. "We kicked his ass, didn't we?" Monique said. I shook my head and I walked into the bathroom while she and Dad talked about what happened.

I looked into the mirror and for the first time, I didn't like what I saw. I looked beaten and defeated. My lip was swollen, I had a large laceration across my lip, and my left eye was swollen shut. I looked like I was in a Mike Tyson fight, and I got TKO'd. That night I promised myself that it wouldn't ever happen again. I got into the gym, and I even took self-defense classes. There was no way I was going back to being the same person I once was, and that is, weak, gullible, and needy. I lost a total of one hundred and ten pounds, and April was back.

CHAPTER FIVE

Gaining Strength And Confidence

"Damn, so you went through all that shit with that man?" Rochelle asked. "I had no idea that you went through something like that, and man was he disrespectful as hell," Silvia said. "I would've never known and after all that you lost all that weight and he was a toxic asshole," Amanda said while in shock.

"Ladies, when I tell you it was hell getting rid of that man, but once I did with the help of my sister Monique and my Dad, I started working out and eating healthy, and I got myself back," I said. "Yes, I see, I can't believe you were that big and you lost all that weight," Silvia said. "Your Dad, kicked his ass good, huh?" Rochelle said. "It sure sounds like it," Amanda said. "Did he ever try to come back?"

Silvia asked. "No, that no good son-of-a-bitch knew better, and right after that, I bought a gun and I intend on taking some self-defense classes shortly just in case that punk got froggy," I said. "I know that's right," Rochelle said. "Your ass wasn't playing," Amanda said. "And, girl, neither should you, don't you take that man back, especially after he put your ass in the hospital and almost killed you," I said. "She better not, because if she does, I am going to kick her ass myself," Silvia said. "I am not taking him back, hell knaw," Amanda said with her half smile.

By the night's end, I was hoping I was getting through to all my girls, but who knows? A person will say anything in front of you and then turn around and go through the same dumb shit anyway.

After the girls left, I took a bath and then I got into my comfortable clothes and lay across my bed. All that bad shit started coming back to me. I couldn't believe I went through all that drama. I wanted to black out that part of my life so badly. I guess telling the girls what happened to me opened up old wounds, but I wasn't going to let it get the best of me, I was exhausted, so I just took my ass to sleep.

I was awakened in the middle of the night by my urges. I kept dreaming about sex and some man making good, good, love to me. My pussy was so wet, and I was so damn horny. I swear sometimes, not having a man in your bed can be the worst on a sister, but damn, I don't want all that stress, but I need some good dick. I rubbed on my pussy until I couldn't take it anymore, and I fell back to sleep. I woke up that next Saturday morning and my urge somehow found its way back into my bed. This time I tried to fight it as I ran a hot tub of water with some good, scented bubble bath. I sat in the hot water and tried to relax, but my pussy kept on pulsating.

At that point, I had no other choice but to play with her until I bust a nut and let me tell you, it felt so damn good to release, but I still wish it was a man who did it.

I felt like jumping back into my bed, but I knew I had to get some things done, plus, I wanted to get to the gym and this new self-defense class. I started my laundry first. As I was folding some clothes, my phone rang.

"Hey April, it's me, girl, what shut the hell up, I am not talking to a man, I am talking to my friend April, oh sorry girl, Benard is tripping again."

"Damn, I was like what, who is Rochelle talking to, ha, ha, I knew it wasn't me, now what is Benard tripping about now?"

"His ass is always tripping, hell, I should be the one tripping, this man can't keep a job to save his damn life."

"You already knew that shit, so why are you still with him?" "It's not that simple." "Are you two married?" "No, hell no," "Then girl, it's just that simple, you just don't want to go." "That's not true, some parts of me want to move on but damn girl, that dick is driving me crazy, I mean he is fucking me up a wall and shit." "TMI, girl, then if it's all about good dick, then don't complain and keep going through the same shit over and over, and please keep me out of y'all toxic ass relationships."

"My relationship isn't toxic, and everybody isn't as strong as you are, April." "That's bullshit, you are just in love with the dick, but I promise you, there is some more good dick out there and they come with a man who's working." "Well, hell, where is he?" "You'll never find him if you don't let Benard go." "I know, I know, what, what, I said hold up, I am coming now, oh sorry, April, Benard is making a fuss about me cooking breakfast." "You are so stupid, tell that muthafucka to cook it himself, I just can't with you, Rochelle, let me get off this phone, maybe one day you'll wake up."

"Let me go," Rochelle said. "Get the fuck off the phone," Benard yelled in the background. "Bye," I said as the ringtone sounded. I do believe one day Rochelle will learn her lesson, but all I can do for now is give her advice, but truthfully, I hate getting into those hoes' business, hell I have my problems.

I finished all of my chores in the house and then I showered and got dressed for the gym. When I made it to the gym, I started working out on my legs. I looked in the mirror at my ass and my hips and I marveled at how much weight I lost up until this point. I couldn't believe I lost 110 pounds. I turned to the side as I stared at myself in the mirror and all I could do is smile as I caught a handsome ass man staring at me through the mirror on the sly. I saw him but I acted like I didn't. I just kept on working out until I started sweating profusely.

Just as I was finishing up my workout, the same guy that I saw staring at me walked up to me and asked if I was done with the bench.

"Oh yes, sure, I am just finishing up," I said.

"Okay, thank you."

"Let me clean it first," I said as I headed for the cleaner.

"That's okay, I trust you."

"Are you sure?"

"I will clean it," "Okay then," I said as I grabbed my towel to wipe the sweat from my face. "Enjoy the rest of your workout." He said as I nodded my head. "You too," I said as I smiled.

Soon as I walked out of the gym, I stopped and smiled as I said aloud, "Damn, that man was fine, and I mean fine, fine."

I could see him watching me as I walked to my car. I hope I see him again. I drove off and headed to the new self-defense class on the other side of town.

"This must be it right here," I said as I pulled up to the Right Am Way strip mall. The sign said, Don't be a Victim, Full Force Self Defense Academy. I admit, I was a bit nervous, but this course will protect me in the future, I was all in.

I got out of my car and started to walk inside, but I was immediately stopped by a well-dressed man. "Excuse me, Miss, may I have a second of your time, please?"

"What is this about?"

"Oh, I am James Larson, and I was wondering if you're single?"

"Am I alone sir?"

"Far as I can see."

"Then yes, I am very single and why do you want to know?"

"I just pulled up into the plaza and as I was getting out of my car, you caught my eye." "Oh, did I, and how is that, because I am all sweaty and in my workout clothes?"

"It's not the clothes, I guess it was just your strong aura."

"Well thank you for the small talk, but I have to get into my new self-defense class."

"For real, is this your first time signing up here?"

"Yes, it is, you are nosy."

"I am so sorry, I am just intrigued, besides, I own this Plaza and I am the self-defense instructor at Full Force Self-Defense Academy, well I own that too."

I must admit, I felt like pure shit. I was a little mean to this guy and turns out he is the one who will teach me self-defense.

"Oh, damn, I am so embarrassed, I didn't know, I thought you were just some random guy."

"That's okay, maybe I should've introduced myself properly."

"No, that was my bad, I am just used to assholes, coming up to me with a lot of game and drama."

"Well, let's start over, I am James Larson and your name?"

"I am April, and it's a pleasure, oh no, I mean it's an honor to meet you, Sir."

Same here, shall we go inside?"

"Yes, let's go," I said as I felt so damn small. I followed him into the establishment, and he showed me where to sign up and he pointed me to the lockers.

I went into the locker room and several other women followed me. I found a locker that was close to the door, and I put my bag inside. Some of the ladies started conversations with me, and it seemed like we were all there to learn how to defend ourselves because of toxic ass men.

I thought I went through hell but some of these ladies went through more than I did. It didn't make any sense for all of us good women to fear for our lives from a man who said they loved us.

When it was time to learn, each one of us was ready to go that extra mile, just to make sure no man was going to ever put his damn hands on us again. Mr. James Larson was a great instructor and he taught me a lot in just that first session.

"Okay, everyone, you all did well today, until next week, just practice what I've taught you, and will get deeper into defense courses next time, okay, good night, everyone." James Larson said.

I started walking towards the locker room and he watched me until I came back out and then he approached me. "Will you be coming back next week?"

"Of course, I will, I enjoyed your class, and I learned a lot," I said with a big smile on my face.

"That's good, and I…" James said as he was interrupted by a woman named Betty. She started trying to get all in his face with her big ass saggy tities. I moved out of the way and turned my nose up. I couldn't believe that bitch was being so rude.

"Okay, I will see you in the session," I said as I slowly walked away. "Okay, okay, we will talk soon, I mean, I will see you in the next session," James said as more women from the class approached him. He smiled for a second as he watched me walk away. I turned back and I smiled at him also. I felt so good leaving the class with a little more knowledge. I knew I was making sure I could protect myself at all costs.

As I drove away, I couldn't stop thinking about that bitch Betty and the way she stepped in front of me and interrupted our conversation, now that's what I call a thirsty ass woman. One day, she's going to get exactly what she deserves, especially if she disrespects me like that again.

I admit that shit was crazy, but I kind of got a sense that Mr. James Larson had more that he wanted to say to me, maybe next time. I made my way home, and for the first time, I felt excited about the change.

CHAPTER SIX

Loving On Myself

    I continued working out and training in the self-defense classes and I even tried to talk the girls into joining but they all made excuses, so I stopped asking. I was beginning to feel good about myself and I felt stronger. There was no way in hell was I going back to that insecure, weak woman, and that made me just feel ecstatic.

    Now that I was starting to feel good about myself again, I knew the only thing missing from my life was being a good man. See here's the thing, you can change yourself, but you can't change anybody else, especially a man, they must be willing to change themselves, so I knew prayer was in order. I wanted a man who was ready mentally, I knew that was a stretch, but I let the one above take control of that, I was only a willing vessel.

I made sure I didn't pray for just a man, but I did pray for a man who was prepared to play his role in my life as a man and not a little boy and I emphasized that I wanted someone ready mentally and stable. Sometimes, you have to watch how you pray and what you pray for, so never just pray for just, a man, I had to learn that the hard way.

Things were now changing in my life, and I loved the direction it was taking. I felt so good about my next journey, just like I decided to go back to school many years ago. I had been a CNA long enough at the nursing home. I was tired of dealing with the hoes and their drama, everybody fucking everybody and even the married folks, hell, they were the worse.

I remember taking online courses and that was the best thing I ever did. I wanted to become an RN, and I was prepared at that time for that upgrade in my life. I was so adamant about that change and here I am once again, making things happen for me.

I constantly went out and I treated myself to a pedicure and I spent a lot of time in the spa getting massages and the works. These messages were the bomb. My shopping therapy increased, especially since I lost so much weight, I had to buy lots of new clothes that fit my new curves. My waist had gotten so small, but my ass and hips didn't seem to go anywhere, so it was hard finding clothes to fit, but I managed to get to the right stores, the ones with an in-house seamstress, that is, ha, ha. "Damn, I am fine," I said as I stood in the mirror trying on a new pair of blue jeans with a gold tie in the front blouse. I turned to the right and left, and I swear, honey, I marveled at my beauty. I couldn't believe how I let a man bring down my self-esteem. I promised myself never to go again.

I stayed consistent in the gym and each time, I found myself being watched by that fine man, I had been seeing there for a while now. It felt like his eyes were staring at me as if I was naked or something. I just kept working out. The staring was starting to get a bit much, but you can't help someone's attraction to you. I mean if he wanted to talk to me, he would say so, because I am not walking up to any man and starting a conversation, that's a man's job, not mine.

After about three months, I started to think this guy was strange because all he did was stare. I got so uncomfortable one day, that I just cut my workout short. He was staring all up in my asshole.

I left with an uneasy feeling, and I headed to my self-defense class. On my way there, I had to make a construction detour through downtown. As I pulled up to the light, I glanced to the left and I saw my ex, Victor, standing and waiting on a bus. All I could do was shake my head. He kept looking at my car, but I turned my head, and I kept looking straight.

As soon as the light turned green, I hurried and pulled off. He put his head down. I wasn't sure if he noticed it was me, but I, sure enough, recognized his ass. He was dirty-looking. Hard times must have caught up with his ass. Seeing him this way, I would never talk to his ass again. "I wonder if he even realized it was me?" But who the fuck cares, I am over that user and loser.

I made it to the self-defense class, and I was so eager to learn new moves and techniques on how to whoop a man's ass, ha, ha. After a grueling class, my instructor, Mr. James, got into a conversation about carrying firearms. I told him I had my gun and permit, and he was elated.

"That's good, so do I, maybe we can go out to the range together and shoot one day?"

"Mr. James Larson, are you asking me out on a date?" I whispered.

"Uhmm, I guess that was a date, ha, ha."

"I do need more practice on using my firearm," I said as I giggled.

"Okay, just let me know when you are available, no pressure at all." He said.

"Will do, I have to go now, I will see you at our next session," I said as I left out the front door.

"Did that man ask me out on a date?" I asked myself as I got into my car with a smile on my face.

By the time I made it home I was so exhausted, I mean I was worn out. I hurried up and showered and then put on my lotion and perfume and I got in bed naked. I didn't even bother to put clothes on.

The next morning, I jumped up to go to work. When I got there the girls were waiting for me. "Hey April, how was your weekend?" Silvia asked. "It was good, it was interesting," I said. "Don't tell me, you told another man's ass off?" Rochelle said. "Maybe, maybe not, if I did then they deserved it," I said. "April, you don't play around, you be like, fuck that shit," Amanda said. "Yes, I do, and you should be the same way, so are you girls okay, what's going on with your relationships?" I asked and everybody got quiet.

"Girl, I am in control of my relationship," Rochelle said.

"Bitch, since when?" Silvia said.

"Since, I said so, Benard knows who's the boss," Rochelle said.

"Now, what's up with your situation, Sylvia?" I asked.

"Old dude, want us to get married," Sylvia said.

"What's wrong with that?" Amanda asked.

"You don't want to know, that is a long story, now isn't Sylvia?" I asked.

"It's none of y'all business," Sylvia said.

"Damn, don't be so damn evil, we are happy for you, but it seems as if you aren't even happy for yourself, what's up with that?" Rochelle said.

Sylvia looked at me and I started back. I know the truth, but the other girls don't. I hurried up and got off that topic because I could tell Sylvia was starting to feel embarrassed and angry at the same time.

"Amanda, what's up with you, you are still staying away from that narcissist, right?" I asked.

"Of course, I am, shit, I can't stand any more drama." She said. For some reason, she didn't sound convincing of herself. I just shook my head and left it alone.

"Hey girls, guess what?" I said. They all said what at the same time.

"I think I was asked on a date," I said with a smile.

"You were, and what did you say, hell no?" Amanda asked.

"Well, no, I am not that mean, am I?" I asked.

"Hell yeah, I am not surprised you didn't hurt that man's feelings," Rochelle said.

"My instructor that I told you girls about, he asked me to go out to the gun range with him," I said.

"That isn't a date, hell who wants to do that, did you tell him, you haven't had a dick in a long time, and you just want to fuck?" Rochelle said,

"Rochelle, that's harsh," Sylvia said.

"No, it's not, now let her answer the damn question," Rochelle said.

"Girl, you are stupid, so, you told him yes?" Amanda asked.

"I told him, I would go some time, but to answer your question, Rochelle, I didn't say all that, but my pussy wanted to, girl he is sexy and fine as his, or did I forget to say he's strong too?" I said as the girl started laughing.

"Well about time, now maybe after y'all shoot those guns maybe he'll shoot his big gun in you, ha, ha," Rochelle said.

"You are so nasty," Amanda said.

"That's all she thinks about?" Sylvia said.

"What's wrong with that?" Rochelle asked as she put both hands up in the air with a puzzled look on her face.

Girl, I have to get to work, I will talk to y'all later." I said.

"We all want some dick, right?" Rochelle said as we just left her standing there looking clueless.

Around lunchtime, Sylvia emailed me, and she said she wanted to talk to me. It sounded serious, the way that she worded the email. I knew she had herself in a bind because she was dating that skinny man, but she was seeing a woman also. I emailed her back and told her it would be good for us to get together after work.

We all met up at lunchtime at the pizzeria down the street from work. After ordering our pizza, I told the girls about the guy at the gym and how he was always staring at me.

"Oooh, you better watch him April, he sounds like he's a weirdo," Sylvia said.

"Maybe he just likes you, and he's just too shy," Amanda said.

"You might be right, maybe I am overanalyzing it," I said.

"You are just scared of dick, just admit it," Rochelle said.

"Girl shut up," Amanda said.

"I am not afraid of any dick, hell, I feel sorry for the man that finally gets the pussy after all this time because, I am going to ride it, like a rodeo," I said, and we all started laughing.

As soon as we finished eating, we headed back to work. The afternoon flew by, and I was starved. We all walked out to the parking lot together and got into our cars. "See you, girls, later," Rochelle said.

"Y'all take it easy, I will see y'all tomorrow, and don't do anything I wouldn't do," Amanda said.

"I am starved, Sylvia, do you want to go get something to eat from somewhere?" I asked.

"Yeah, I am starved."

"Okay, let's go to Ridge Diner out in Irondequoit," I said.

"Okay, bet, that sounds good, I think I want a steak, a nice, fat, juicy steak," Sylvia said.

"What are you two talking about?" Rochelle said.

"I think they are talking about food," Amanda said.

"Yall is some greedy ass hoes," Rochelle said.

"Who are you calling a hoe, it takes a hoe to know a hoe, ha, ha," I said as I rolled up my window. Rochelle had a sour-looking face after I put her ass on blast.

Sylvia and I met out at the Ridge Diner, and we ordered our food. I started talking about what was wrong with her. And, it turns out, she's in love with that skinny man and that woman Amesia.

That damn girl got herself in a bind. Deep down she doesn't want anyone to know she likes women, but she just doesn't want to be without a man either. Truthfully, I didn't know what to tell her, but I did say, "If you just want a man because of what others say you should be with then you won't ever be happy, you have to be with the one you love no matter what."

Even with my advice, she still couldn't make up her mind. She was in love with both of them and there wasn't anything I could say, hell, I am not a therapist.

After getting nowhere at all with Sylvia, we parted ways as we left the Ridge Diner. I headed home and jumped out of my clothes, and I walked around butt-ass naked. It felt good to be home.

As I made myself a glass of wine, I started feeling all warm and tingly inside, so I decided to take a hot shower. I got out and I started feeling horny and my pussy started pulsating. I reached under my bed and pulled out my toys. I took another sip of my wine and lay back on my bed and oi started rubbing in a circular motion on my clit. My pussy got so wet as I stuck one and then two fingers inside of me. I started moaning and squirming as I began to please myself.

My legs started trembling as I pulled out my dildo and I stuck just the head of it inside of me. I had to catch myself as I felt the pressure from the insertion. My mouth opened wide; I took a deep gulp. My juices gushed out and started running down both of my inner thighs. I

CHARLES LEE ROBINSON JR.

couldn't stop my body from having convulsions as I stuck the dildo deeper inside my pussy. I started loving myself as I exploded on my sheets with my hot juices. I rubbed my breast and squeezed both of my nipples as pleasure and passion took over me. It felt so good to release and bust a nut as hard as I did, but again, I wish it was a man giving me these deep, tunneling pleasures. Loving myself is the best!

CHAPTER SEVEN

Dating Has Changed

After not having a man for so long, I thought it was time that I started dating again. I was new to what was going on out there in the world. I didn't want to seem thirsty, because I am still a lady, but it seemed if I had to make the first move, then so be it. This was out of the norm for me, but I must admit, the urges were starting to get the best of me.

While working out in the gym that guy who had been staring at me walked by me and he smiled. That was the first time I had seen him show a cute little smile like that. So, I felt like I should finally say something.

"Hello, how are you, I am April."

"Oh, hi, I am Cedric." He said softly.

"It's nice to meet you."

"Same here, I thought you were too mean to speak."

"Huh, what, I thought you were too shy to speak."

"Now why would you think that, so I look mean?"

"Ha, ha, uhm, yes."

"Damn, I have to change that, ha, ha," I said as I giggled.

"I guess I have to change that shy look also, well it's a pleasure to meet you." He said.

Yes, yes, it's definitely a pleasure." I said.

Cedric and I started working out together every day, but in the meantime, my instructor James was still asking me out to the gun range or just any date.

Since I was single, I decided that I would go on dates with both of them. As time went on, I met two more guys, one named Alonzo and the other named Robert. I guess I was trying to see who would better fit me.

I think at first, I was truly feeling Cedric, but he seemed like he was always too busy, plus being a gym rat and all. I didn't want to fight for his time, so after a few dates, I told him it was best that we just stayed friends and that we could occasionally work out together.

He stopped speaking to me the very next time that I saw him in the gym. Hey, it wasn't my loss. At least I said we could still be friends. I left the gym, confused. I needed to work off some stress, so I did just that in my self-defense class.

"Hey, April, are you okay, I see you are letting everybody have it that you spare with, I know I have insurance but hey. Don't kill everyone, ha, ha." James said and we both started laughing.

"Was I that bad, I am sorry?" I said as I dropped my head. "Don't be sorry, listen my offer still stands, whenever you are ready, we can go out and talk about whatever is bothering you, okay?"

"Okay, I will let you know," I said as I left the class. I know he keeps asking me out, but I just don't know why I haven't accepted his offer yet, maybe I am scared of something real, I don't know!

I decided to give Alonzo a try. We went out on a date. It was so nice at first. We went for a walk near the Lilacs in the park and then we went to a matinee movie. We had so much in common. Our date was going so well that we decided to meet for dinner that evening.

We met at the Long House Steak Restaurant. As I pulled up, he walked up to my car and waited for me. In my mind, I was thinking, "Aren't you going to open the door for me?" Unfortunately, that never happened, and I had to open my door myself. That was the first red flag. So, of course, I had just a little attitude as the waiter took us to our seats, I walked slowly as Alonzo just walked all fast in front of me.

"Are you okay, April, you seem like you're in a funky ass mood?" I tried to stay quiet about this situation, "I am okay, don't worry about it." "Okay, man, I am so hungry, you got this meal right, it's on you this time?" He said. I looked at him like he was crazy.

"Sure, why, don't you have any money?" I asked with an attitude.

"Yes, I am just playing, can't you take a joke, I was just messing with you, are you sure you are fine?"

"I am okay, I was just playing with you also," I said sarcastically. Alonzo started looking at the menu and he did not once look into my eyes.

"Are you okay, that's the question that I should be asking you, Alonzo?" "I am okay, I am just hungry." He said.

"I see, I can tell that, the way you beat me to the seat, and you didn't open my door to my car."

"Oh, I did that, my bad." He said without a care. I looked at his big, strong, muscles popping out of his shirt, and I said to myself, "This muthafucka looks good for nothing."

"Are you okay, are you ready to order, or do you want me to order for you?"

"No, I can order for myself, thank you," I said as I rolled my eyes at him while sticking my head into the menu. At that point, I didn't see any reason to keep on the date, but I hated to just leave like that. I was so happy when Alonzo asked me to excuse him so he could go to the restroom because he was beginning to get on my damn nerves. It's bad enough that I promised myself that I wouldn't let another man ruin my damn peace.

I started to leave then but my conscience was eating at me. Alonzo came back and sat down. "Did the waiter come while I was gone?" "Yes, he did, and I told him to give us a second because you were in the bathroom."

"Wow, they don't waste any time, I guess."

"I guess not, I mean you were in the bathroom for about five minutes or so, you must have been on the phone texting another chick, ha, ha," I said.

"That's not funny, no, no, I wasn't." He said seriously.

"Relax, calm down, I was only kidding."

"That didn't sound like you were kidding, maybe this date was a bad idea."

"I said I was just playing, but maybe you are right, I am about to go, this isn't working."

"Yeah, I don't want to waste my money on someone who has bad jokes anyway.

"You know what, you snooty muthafucka, eat by yourself muscle man," "Goodbye and good riddance." He said with an attitude.

"Good, and by the way, you're all muscular and shit, but I can tell by the print in your pants that you have a little dick and so is your brain, see ya," I said, and I walked out of the restaurant.

I glance back as I was leaving, and I could see Alonzo looking down at his little dick. Even though I was pissed the hell off, I couldn't do anything but laugh as I jumped into my car.

I felt so good leaving the parking lot. He had the looks, but his personality didn't fit mine. I am not settling anymore, and that's why I knew I had to get out of there. That was a lesson learned. I won't tolerate a disrespectful man, hell, I know how to fuck myself when I get a little horny.

For a couple of weeks, I just stayed to myself. I was thinking about not dating anyone at this point. But every hour, Robert would call me and check up on me.

"Hey there, how are you doing April, when are we going on a date?"

"I am not sure; I just haven't been in the mood lately;"

"It's my treat, you don't have to worry about that."

"It's not about the partying part, I can buy my own dinner or meal, I've just been in a funk lately and I just don't want to be bothered."

"Bothered, bothered, I didn't think I was bothering you, look, I can tell you've been through a lot, I am only here to make you feel better and take some of the stress off you."

"I get it, but now, isn't the time, can we chat later?"

"Sure, sure, okay, I hope you have a good night."

"You too, good night, Robert," I said as I hung up the phone. I knew I was being a little rude to Robert, but I wasn't in the mood for small talk.

Day after day he checked on me. I would answer the phone and talk to him for a little while. He was kind of cool and he kept my spirits up.

"So, are you okay today?" He asked.

"Yes, I am okay, thanks for asking, and yourself?"

"I am doing just fine, especially to know you are doing well.

"Really, now why are you so nice to me?"

"Why, I shouldn't be?"

"I am only curious."

"As I said, I can tell you are going through something, and I just want to be here for you."

"That's sweet but I am a big girl, I will be all right."

"I don't have any doubts about that, why are you seeing someone?"

"No, why, if I was, I wouldn't be talking to you."

"You are only talking to me because I call you all the time."

"Well, I am a woman, and I am not supposed to chase a man."

"Who said anything about chasing a man, I am only saying, I am interested in you, I show you because I call and check on you, how do I know you feel the same, I mean how would I know?"

"First of all, you are not my man, I don't have to call you, you are the hunter, not me, the only time I would call you, and that's if you were my man, but to answer your other question, you will know if interested by you calling and I pick up the phone and answer it, Hun, I don't chase any man, I am sorry, you have the wrong chick."

"Damn, it's like that, I mean I wasn't insisting that you had to call me, I was only curious, wow, somebody hurt you badly, but please don't take it out on me."

"I am not talking out anything on you, you asked me a couple of questions and I answered them, so nope, I won't be calling you unless you are my man."

"How could we even get to that point, if you don't even try?"

"Try what, I told you, I don't want to be bothered, you are cool and all, but I just can't."

"Then you shouldn't have given me your number, you're right, I shouldn't have bothered you, have a good night."

"Good night," I said as I slammed the phone. I could tell he was a clingy ass dude, and I want another man, not another pussy, boy bye.

I was so pissed off at men at this point, so I didn't see the need to keep dating, so I thought. One day after self-defense class, I went out to get into my car and my tire was flat.

"Ahh, damn, my tire is flat, shit, shit, shit, shit," I said as I stomped my feet.

"April are you okay?" James said as he walked up.

"Yes, and no, look my tire is flat, and now it's going to take hours for Triple AAA to come, I am so pissed.

"Don't be, it happens to us all, if you have a spare tire, I will fix it for you and let you be on your way.

"Will you do that?"

"Of course, now do you have a spare?"

"Uhm, yes, let me open up the trunk," I said as I pulled the trunk latch inside.

Within ten minutes, James fixed my flat and I was so ecstatic.

"Thank you, thank you."

"No need for thanks, that's what friends are for."

"Oh, we are friends now, ha, ha," I said as I giggled.

"I should hope so, we see each other at least three times a week, and you still haven't accepted my date at the gun range, ha, ha." He said as he smiled.

"I will do you one better since you fixed my flat tire, I will go to the gun range with you, and I will pay for our first dinner."

"First dinner, wow, and the gun range, damn, please catch another flat tire, ha, ha." He laughed.

"Ha, ha, now that was funny, I like to thank you again, you name the date and time and we can go out on a date, but I must warn you, I am, a little rusty at this, and my mouth is slick sometimes."

"No worries sometimes my mouth can be a little slick al; so, but it comes with the territory."

"I guess so because you be putting a whooping on us in class, ha, ha."

"I do not, ha, ha, hey, here's my number, but I will call you and then we can work on getting together soon."

"Yes, that sounds good, we will talk later," I said as I got in my car and drove off. I must admit, he made me smile and he made me feel good. I started thinking to myself, why didn't I go out with him a long time ago?"

Anyway, I knew this was the right time and I believe James made me feel good already. After checking our schedules, we made a date to hit the gun range on the weekend.

We both met at the gun range, and we immediately clicked. We couldn't stop laughing and having fun. James kept trying to teach me how to aim my firearm and I kept trying to distract him as he shot his. He was incredibly good, and he hit the targets almost every time.

"Where did you learn how to shoot like that?" I asked.

"I was in the Marines, and they teach you very well."

"I see, I want you to teach me," I said as I shot at the target a few more times and missed.

We both laughed, but he finally walked over to me, and he gave me a few pointers. Before we left the gun range, I was hitting my targets and I winked at James as we were getting ready to leave. I must admit that was so much fun and I enjoyed James's company.

We planned our dinner and then when the time came, we made it happen. Up until now, I hadn't had so much fun, and James was genuinely nice, and intriguing. I learned so much about him, and he even inspired me, so damn, real, I was going to see him and date him again. I hadn't felt like this with a man in so long and he just turned me on, while just being in his presence.

CHAPTER EIGHT

Having The Conversation

After a few months of dating James, I was starting to feel scared because I knew I was getting comfortable with him, and my guard was slowly going down.

We went on so many dates and the talks that we had started to draw me to him slowly and that made my heart quiver. I didn't want another letdown. I wanted to make sure he was someone that I could trust. I knew opening up to him was inevitable.

I decided to open up to the girls one day while we were at lunch, and they were all surprised.

"Say what, you are seeing your instructor, your self-defense instructor, do you think he's packing?" Rochelle asked.

"That's none of your business, you crazy nut," Amanda said. "Here goes Miss Horny-toes again, but is he?" Sylvia said. "You girls are nasty as hell and nosy, mine your business," I said. "You must really like him, especially since you are telling us about him, I thought you were just dating a bunch of guys, ha, ha," Rochelle said. "And, if I did, that's my business," I said. "You don't have to get so feisty," Rochelle said. "Girl, leave her alone, so you like him, don't you?" Amanda asked. "Yes, I do, but a part of me is scared," I said. "Scared of what?" Sylvia said. "She just scared of that dick, ha, ha, that's what she's scared of," Rochelle said, and she started laughing. "Hà, ha, no, I am not." I said as I tried to contain myself while laughing.

We all started laughing and I told them exactly how I felt. "Have you and him had that talk yet?" Amanda asked. "That real talk, that real, real, conversation?" I said. "Yeah, did you tell him you are scared?" Rochelle said sarcastically. "Shut up girl," Sylvia said. "Y'all are too funny," Amanda said as she giggled. "I plan on having a conversation with James soon," I said.

The girls and I talked through lunch, and I felt better after giving them the heads up on James and me. They congratulated me and praised me because they knew that I rarely let my guard down for any man. I believe they kind of felt like this was the real deal and deep down, so did I.

James and I conversed all week and by the weekend we planned to go to the State Fair in Syracuse, New York to spend some time together. I explained to him that we needed to talk because our relationship was starting to get serious.

"Are we staying the weekend here?" I asked. "Sure, what do you think?" "I mean, I want to have fun with you and for us to get in-depth with each other, about what we want from each other, so let's get a room," I said, and a big smile came across James's face. "I mean with double beds," I said with a straight face and his smile slowly disappeared. "Hell, we are grown, let's get the two beds and if something happens, it just happens," I said, and James smiled again.

We found a room at the Hilton Hotel, and it was genuinely nice inside. The hotel clerk said, "How many beds?" We both looked at each other and we said, "Two, please." And we both laughed. "Okay then." The hotel clerk said as she laughed with us.

We put our things in the room, and we decided to go for a walk downstairs in the lobby. There were restaurants on the first floor and a few bars. "James, let's talk." "Okay, what do you want to talk about?"

James asked. "Let's walk over there, it looks quiet," I said. "Do you want me to order us a couple of drinks first?" He asked. "Yes, of course, since the bars are right there, I will have a pink Moscato please," I said with a grin on my face. "Yes, that sounds good, but I need a shot of that Tequila," James said as he licked his lips. "Well go ahead and get your shot, and don't forget my Moscato, please," I said as James headed over to the bar. I went and walked over to a large water fountain which was on the other side of the lobby. The water was sparkling, and I could see the reflection of my face.

Just as I was about to fall into my thoughts, James walked over with my drink. "James, where is your drink?" "I had my shot at the bar." "You drank your drink that quickly?" "Yes, I did, and actually it was a double shot, ha, ha." He said. "A double shot, what are you trying to do, pass out and fall asleep on me?" "No, not at all, I can handle my liquor." "I bet you can, I thought you were at least going to have a toast with me." "If you want us to have a toast, then let me order myself a glass of Merlot." "Yes, please, and that is an excellent choice, hurry, I will wait." "Okay, okay, good, there aren't that many people at the bar," James said as he walked down to the bar.

Moments later, he came with his wine and we both smiled. "Let's make this toast." He said as he put his wine glass in the air. "What are we going to toast to?" "Let's toast, to us, good conversation, a good time, and a toast to the beginning of something new and something special." "Yes, I agree, and that is us, toast," I said as I put my glass up to his. James twirled his hands around mine and put his glass up to mine and he said, "Toast."

We finished our drinks, and we were both feeling nice with a little buzz. "So, how are you feeling tonight?" He asked. "I feel marvelous, especially with being with you, you know, I never thought I would ever feel this comfortable with a man like this ever again." "For real, and why is that?" "Like I've told you about my life in the past, I had it hard and my self-esteem was low." "Yes, I remember you telling me that, it's just so hard to believe, especially seeing how strong you are today, whatever happened to you in the past, is just that, it's the past, and just look at it this way, it turned you into a beautiful and strong woman, you can be an inspiration to other women that went through the same things." "Thank you, that was sweet," I said as we kept walking and talking about our lives.

"James, I've told you about my ex, Victor, and how he made me feel, so you know that it's hard for me to give my all and if I do, I have to know that you or any man will be here for the long haul."

"I understand that, and I have been through some crazy things in my life also, so I know why you still have a wall up, I have one too, so it takes a special woman to get me to open up, and so far, I am, feeling comfortable with you."

"I am feeling comfortable with you also, funny thing, it seems as if we've known each other all of our lives," I said.

"Yes, that's called chemistry, and I would love to be in your life for the long haul, now I don't expect you to just believe the words that are coming out of my mouth because I plan to show you, just that."

"Well, I am glad you are a man of action, and trust me, I will be here for you if you are there for me, I am all about the both of us putting in 100/100 percent because I am not with that 50/50 percent, shit."

"I agree, I can only put in 100 percent and nothing less," James said as he turned and looked into my eyes. I stared back into his eyes, and he grabbed both of my hands. We sat on a bench outside of the lobby, and we sat in silence for about fifteen seconds before we spoke again.

I guess you can say we were into each other, and we wanted our next words to be right, I wanted James to know that as a woman, I have boundaries and expectations, and I let him know I expected to hear his too. I didn't want to be in another relationship where we had to assume we knew what the other was thinking or wanted.

"Look James, I just want you to be honest with me, don't disrespect me, and please don't downgrade me or insult me because I am a queen and I need to be treated as such."

"I would never insult you, or put you down, that's not what I am here for, I want to help you become a better woman, and in return, you help me to be a better man, by far I am not perfect, but I hope you can be there to help me with the things I fall short on."

"I can definitely do that, and just know, no matter what, you can trust me, you can confide in me, communication is the key, please don't hold anything back and we will be all right."

"I am a great communicator, so you don't have to worry about that, and I am loyal, I don't expect you to just hear words, because I will show you that I am the man for you."

"You will, now will you, I like that, keep on sweet-talking me." "Ha, ha, no, I am for real, you have my full attention."

"And, you have my full attention, James, let's get back to the room, I am starting to feel a little exhausted.

"Yes, it has been a long day, plus those shots and the wine are making me feel really good inside."

"Ha, ha, I thought it was just me, come on, are you ready?" "Yes, I am come on, let's go."

"Hey, ha, ha, did you just stumble, now do I have to help you to the room, mister?"

"No, I am, okay, I think I stepped on a pebble or something, ha, ha."

"Ha, ha, a pebble my ass, you better walk straight, ha, ha, you'll be okay, I have your back."

"I am okay, I promise, and, I have your back also," James said as he grabbed my hand, and we headed to the room.

We made it back to the room where there were two beds and we glanced at each other. "I will let you choose which bed you want while I am in the shower." "Okay, that's cool," James said as I grabbed my things, and went into the bathroom.

"I will be right out," I said as I stuck my head out of the bathroom. "Okay, I think I want the bed by the window," James said as I closed the door.

I stood behind the bathroom door and slowly pulled my clothes off. I couldn't help but think about how I was in the presence of a man, and it's been such a long time since I was.

My body started tingling and then my pussy started pulsating as I rubbed on my breast and my soft skin. Deep down inside, I wanted to be strong but the other part of me, wanted James to make love to me. I was so confused and scared at the same time. I knew if I gave myself up to him, I would be giving up my strength.

I wanted to release it so badly, but my mind and my body were saying two different things. "Let me get my horny ass, in this shower," I said to myself. I stood under the water in the shower as the thoughts of some good loving crossed my mind repeatedly. I hadn't had sex or been touched in so long, that I didn't know what to do with myself.

My pussy kept on pulsating, so I had to rub on her as I stood in the shower, I put soap on my entire body. As I lathered up really well, I put two fingers inside of me and exhaled as I could feel the pressure from the insertion. I twirled my fingers inside my pussy, and I started breathing heavily and softly at the same time.

"April are you okay," James yelled out. *His voice startled me because I could hear him as my eyes were closed and my finger slid inside and out of me. My pussy was gushing wet, and I had to stop grinding on my fingers as I answered,* "I will be right out."

I knew at that moment that I had to get control of myself, *so I took my fingers out of my pussy slowly and I began to wash her, and I got all of these wet juices out of me as I inserted my cloth inside of me.*

"I am coming," I yelled as I dried myself off and put on my panties, bra, and my tan silk robe. I walked out and I almost fainted as James stood there in his black boxers with no shirt on. I grasped my breath, and I acted as if I didn't see a thing.

"I will be right out." He said. "Okay," I said as I sat on the bed, and I pulled out my lotion and my perfume. Soon as the bathroom door shut, I screamed silently to myself, "Damn, he is fine, and that body, oh my." *My pussy just got wetter, as I thought of him in that shower with that hot water running down his sexy, and strong-looking body.*

I wanted James so badly, and I couldn't stop my urges, but I tried. When James came out of the bathroom, he was still a little wet and he had his towel wrapped around his waist. I watched him walk over to the other bed and lotion himself. I acted like I wasn't looking as I tucked myself into the other bed. "How do you feel?" He asked. "I feel good, are you refreshed?" "Yes, I feel good." "Well, let me get some rest," I said as I turned on my side in the bed. "Yes, same here, I need some sleep," James said as he turned the other way on the bed.

As I lay there, my body and my mind started taking over me, I knew right then, that I needed James' arms around me. "James, are you asleep?" "No. I am not; I am tired, but I can't sleep." "Me neither, can you come over here and hold me, please?" "Sure," He said as he walked over to my bed.

His body felt so good pressed up to my mine and instantly my pussy got wet, and she started pulsating. I turned around slowly and faced James and we started kissing. The next thing I knew, we were taking off our clothes.

"Do you have any protection?" I whispered. "Yes, I do, let me go get it." "James, I need you to make love to me." "Okay, I want you so bad, you just don't know." He said. "I want you just as much, put your dick inside me, I need to feel you inside of me." "Come here, baby." He whispered delicately and his voice gave me chills. "It is so wet." "Yes, she is so wet, for you, put it, ah, ah," I said as he inserted his *dick inside of me. It was long and it felt as if it had no end. I jumped back a little and James pulled his long dick out of me until only the tip of his dick was in me and then suddenly, he thrust all of it inside me, My eyes widens and my mouth opened broadly, and just like that, I started cumming all over the place and every time he stroked my pussy, I started exploding all over his dick. It felt so good, as I watched him finally cum. I could feel all his convulsions as his orgasm hit my body. I could tell because he stiffened up and he moaned and groaned until it stopped.*

I had waited years for this, and it was everything I had imagined. I was pleased, my pussy was pleased and by the way, James had a big smile on his face afterward, I knew he was pleased.

That was the best weekend I had in my life, and I knew it was something special to be cherished.

CHARLES LEE ROBINSON JR.

CHAPTER NINE

The Direction Of Our Lives

James and I made it back home late Sunday night. He dropped me off at my house. I must admit, I was happy I took that trip, and I was also glad that I got myself some good dick. It was much needed. I got all that stress off me and it made me feel like a new woman.

Just as I was about to get relaxed, I got a phone call from Sylvia. "Hey, April, are you back home for the State Fair?" "Yes, girl, I just got in, James, literally, just dropped me off at home." "What, he's not staying the night?" "Girl, why do you want to know, you are just being nosy." "Since you put it that way, dammit, yes, I am," Sylvia said as she giggled. "We both have early mornings, that's why." "It sounds like you had a good time, I mean I don't hear you complaining." "There isn't anything to complain about, James is a good man, he was fantastic, he was attentive and respectful, and it was a great time." "Damn, he's all that, already, it sounds like somebody is falling in love." "No, I am not in love, but maybe strong like." "Strong like, huh?" "Yes, that's it, strong like." "Bullshit, who you are fooling?" "Sylvia, don't start, I like the guy, okay, now what did you call for?" "I needed advice." "Advice about what?" "I am so confused, I don't want everyone to know that I am bisexual, I love both of my partners, and I don't want to choose one or the other." "What, girl that's crazy, you have to pick one." "I know, I know, but I don't want to pick Amesia because I want to keep my secret."

"You probably just answered your question, you want her, but you don't want to let your secret out, so you are trying to stay with that skinny, ugly man, just to say you got a man so that your secret is kept." "He is not ugly, but yes, I guess that's it, hell, I don't know." "If you don't know, then hell, I don't know either, Sylvia I am tired, I have to go so I can get up in the morning for work, you better figure this shit out yourself." "Okay, bye, you're no help," Sylvia said as she quickly hung up the phone. "That's one confused bitch." I said aloud to myself.

I unpacked my clothes and then I got all my things ready for the work week, after folding all my clothes, I sat on the bed and started thinking about making love to James. It was so good, and I wanted it to happen again. I smiled as I had flashbacks of him and me, getting it on in that hotel bed. I was starting to get wet in between my legs just thinking about it.

Just as I was getting into my thoughts, my phone rang again. "Hello, who is it?" "Hey, April, are you home, I need to get out of this house now," Rochelle yelled.

"Rochelle, what's wrong, are you okay?"

"Hell no, this muthafucka won't leave, and I want him out of here, now." She said.

"Fuck you, I am not going anywhere," Benard said in the background.

"Girl, what's going on with you two?"

"I am tired of his sorry ass, he won't work in a pie factory, he eats all my food, he talks shit, always accusing me of cheating, and then after he insults me and steal my fucking money, he wants to have sex with me, hell no, no more, I want him gone."

"Then why don't you kick him out," I said.

"I tried but the police said since he gets mail here, and his name is on the mailbox, I can't kick him out unless I evict him."

"What kind of crazy shit is that, you have had your house for fifteen years or so, and they can't make him leave?"

"No, they said I have to take him to court, I am so miserable, why won't he go, I want him gone, now," Rochelle shouted.

"I'm not going anywhere; you heard what the police said, now what, fuck you, make me leave," Benard said loudly.

"Girl, you got yourself in some shit, you should've left his sorry ass a long time ago, I told you, I already went through this shit, but never again, I won't ever stay with another man just to say I have one," I said with anger in my voice,

"I don't know what I am going to do."

"What much can you do, I bet the next time, you won't let a muthafucka stay up in your house,"

"Hell no, this is it, a lesson learned, damn, I want to fuck his ass up, but I don't want to go to jail and let him be laying here, up in my shit, with another bitch." She said.

"I hear that, well you better go down to the courthouse and start the paperwork so you can evict his ass."

"I will, damn, how did I get myself in this shit?"

"It was that good dick, it will steer you wrong every time especially if it's on the wrong man, be safe, I have to get off the phone, I am exhausted, plus, I just got in the house from my trip," I said,

"That's right, okay, we will talk tomorrow, and I will handle that court shit after work, bye, I will talk to you, later."

"Okay, be careful, bye," I said as we hung up the phone. I hated hearing that Rochelle was going through all that drama, it just reminded me of what I had to get through. It was sort of similar. And, that's something I could never deal with again. I hope she isn't all talk, and she finally kicks his ass out. The nerve of these narcissistic men. There's no way in hell, I could ever put up with that kind of shit in my life.

That night, I knew I had to pray for my girl, Rochelle. That's an awful way to live your life. A man comes a dime a dozen, but you only get one life. I was so worried about her that I couldn't even sleep. For some reason, I wanted to check on Amanda. I know she was also going through some tough times. After talking to Rochelle, I had to make sure Amanda didn't take that crazy ass man back, he'd already beat her ass once and put her in the hospital.

I called Amanda repeatedly but no answer. I started to get scared because that's not like her to answer her phone that late at night. I called several more times, but still no answer. I hung up the phone and started to walk into the bathroom and then my phone rang.

"Hello, who is this?" I asked.

"Hey, April, it's Amanda, did you call me?"

"Yes, I called you several times, I was worried about you."

"Worried about me, why?"

"Never mind, it's a long story, did you talk to the girls?" I asked so I could change the subject. "No, I haven't, have been busy." "Too busy to talk to your girls?" "No, not like that, I was just reflecting." "Reflecting about what?" I asked and for a few seconds, Amanda went silent. "Amanda, are you okay, what's going on?" "Oh, nothing, like I said I was only reflecting." She said with a pause.

"Has that crazy ass man contacted you again?" I asked and she paused before she spoke again.

"Girl, no, no, so, how was your weekend?" Amanda said as if making small talk.

"Are you sure there isn't anything wrong?" I asked once more.

"No, not at all, I guess your weekend was good, I hope you tell me about it tomorrow at work." She said.

"Most definitely, okay, let me get off this phone, I am so exhausted, we will chat tomorrow, bye."

"Bye, April, I will talk to you tomorrow," Amanda said with a pause. After I hung up the phone, I felt uneasy. I sure hope she hasn't gotten back with that crazy ass man who physically and mentally abused her, she sure seemed a little secretive.

I must admit, it's so hard watching your friends go through some of the same shit you had to go through and there isn't anything you can do about it but give them good advice.

I hope and pray I don't ever have a man disrespect me and treat me like I am not worthy. I am a Queen, I am a good woman and I deserve better, hell every woman deserves it.

I sat on my bed, and I thought how lucky I was to meet a guy like James. I know he isn't perfect, but I can feel deep down in my heart, he has my best interest at heart. I never want to go back to being that overweight, insecure woman who lets a man get away with everything he wants just so I can say I have someone, hell I don't want or need a piece of man. I am a real woman and I deserve a real man.

As I got ready for bed, I prayed for all my friends, and I lay across my bed just thinking. As soon as I was about to close my eyes, my phone rang once again.

"Hello, who is it?" "It's me, James, I was just calling to say goodnight, but I didn't think you were still up, I was just about to leave a message. "I was just about to close my eyes, ha, ha, or I did close my eyes, thank you so much, and thank you for the weekend."

"Anytime, I hope you sleep well, good night, and I hope to see you in class, ha, ha," James said. "Yeah right, you beat me up in a good way this past weekend, I need a few days off." "Ha, ha, okay me too, goodnight baby." "Good night, James," I said as I hung the phone up slowly, soon after thinking about our weekend, I fell asleep.

CHAPTER TEN

Life Will Throw You A Curveball

The next morning, I was tired as hell, but I got my ass up anyway to get ready for work. I did my usual routine as I showered, put lotion on my body, and got dressed.

I admired the beautiful curves on my body as I fixed my blouse and pulled up my rust-colored pants as I marveled at myself in my mirror. There is something about good sex that brings a certain glow to a woman.

I pushed myself out of the door and proceeded to head to work. Funny thing as I was on my way to work, my sister Monique and my mother called me back-to-back. They wanted to know how I was doing, so I had to tell them the truth, and I did mention James.

My mother gave me a whole lecture. "Are you sure you are ready for another relationship; you know that last man you had was crazy as hell." "Well, I am not sure, but James seems to be different," I said. "They all seem to be different at first." "This is true, Mom, I am just going to take it one day at a time." "Okay, just be careful, men aren't shit these days." "Mom," "Mom. Hell, shit, I am telling the truth, just be careful because next time it won't just be your Dad kicking ass, I will be there too, with my butcher knife." "Mom, no need for that, besides, James teaches self-defense, I don't even think Dad, can handle him or your rusty butcher knife." "Damn, you got a tough man, well, I still have my gun, ha, ha." "Ha, ha, Mom, stop it, James, isn't like that, besides, I have a gun also and he has taught me a lot of different moves, he better not make me use his shit on him, ha, ha, let me stop." "Ha, ha, I know, I am taking it too far, but I will do anything for my baby, aren't you at work?" "No, not yet, but I am on my way." "Okay, April, I will talk to you later, bye." "Bye, Mom," I said.

My sister Monique was more negative. She acted as if I shouldn't talk to any man. She sounded like she despised men, but I understood it was because of her bad experiences with men in her relationships. I assured her that James was different, but she wasn't hearing anything I said. "Okay Sis, if you say so, don't make me have to call Dad, again." "And, about you calling Dad." "Bye," Monique said as she hung up the phone hastily.

"That damn, girl hung up on me, her crazy ass," I said to myself. I can understand them worrying about me, but I am a grown-ass woman and I know better now. I won't let another man bring me down ever again.

I made it to work at the perfect time after talking to my Mom and sister. "Hey, April, what's going on, I bet you had fun, fun," Rochelle said as she met me in the parking lot.

"Let's just say, that thang still works, ha, ha."

"Oh, yeah, you got yourself some dick, and that old rusty thing still works, ha, ha."

"Rusty, hell, anyways, hey Sylvia," I said with a smile on my face.

"Good morning girls," Sylvia said as she walked up to us after stepping out of her car.

"Where is Amanda, has anyone talked to her?" I asked.

"No, I called her all weekend, but no answer," Rochelle said.

"That's odd, I called her too," Sylvia said.

"That is odd, well maybe she's coming in late," I said as we all walked into work.

The day was going well, but there was still no Amanda. I tried calling her several times that morning. Finally, I got a text from her around noon, and she said, "Hey April, I had to stay home today, something came up." The text was strange to me, so I asked, "Are you okay, is everything all right?" After my text, she didn't reply right away. I decided to call Ms. Brooks, Amanda's mother.

"Ms. Brooks, how are you doing this afternoon?" "Hey, April I am, doing fine, so what's going on?"

"Nothing much, I am doing great, I was just wondering if you talked to your daughter Amanda lately?"

"Not as much as I would like, Amanda, has been seeming estranged lately, I am not sure what's going on with her, but she never answers her phone or texts, and if she does, it takes her a long time to respond."

"That's exactly what I and the girls have been getting from her lately."

"I sure hope, she isn't back with that no good, crazy ass man."

"I sure hope not also, for her sake, well if you talk to her or see her, please talk some sense into her," I said.

"I will, even if I have to knock some sense in her head, she had better not have taken that man back, he damned near killed her last time and it was hard seeing my baby in the hospital like that, plus fighting for her life." Ms. Brooks said with passion and pain in her voice.

"I understand completely, I sure hope Amanda is smarter than that," I said.

"Okay, well, I will talk to you later, and I will keep you posted, please do the same."

"I definitely will, Ms. Brooks," I said as I exhaled.

"Okay, I will talk to you later, and April, thanks for calling me."

"You are welcome, I will talk to you later," I said as I closed my eyes, and I did a short prayer for Amanda. I continued to work until the end of the day. After doing all my rounds at the hospital, Amanda finally replied in a text.

"I am okay, everything is good, thanks for checking up on me."

"Are you, I mean really, are you sure you are all right?" I texted and then I didn't get a reply. I left work that day feeling strange. I knew deep down in my soul that something was wrong.

I had to confide in someone about the issue, so I called James as I pulled up into my driveway. "Hi, James, do you have a few minutes to talk?" "I sure do, for you, do you want me to come by your house?" "Yes, please, I need you," I said as I was so exhausted. "I will be there in about an hour." He said.

I walked into the house and started cleaning up. After that, I jumped out of my clothes and got into the shower. I put on my gown, and I was too tired to put on my panties and bra, this day drained the hell out of me. Soon as I got refreshed my doorbell rang.

"Who is it?" I yelled. "It's me, James." I ran to the door and grabbed my see-through robe with no panties on," "Coming." I yelled.

I opened the door and a huge smile came across my face. "Well, hello, sexy," James said as a huge smile came across his face.

"Oops, I didn't mean to come to the door like this."

"Ha, ha, like what, all sexy you mean, see-through with nothing under, hmmm, yeah, okay," James said as he looked me up and down while licking his lips.

"Don't you start, we will definitely get to that, but I need to talk to you about something that has been bothering me." "Okay, sure, now, on a more serious note, what's wrong?" "Come over here and sit on the sofa, would you like anything to drink?" "Sure, just water." "Okay water, sure, let me get you a cold bottle out of the fridge," I said as I walked into the kitchen.

I handed James a cold bottle of water and sat down, I told him all about my friends and what they were going through, especially how I was worried about Amanda.

"I don't mean to sound heartless but April, sometimes you have to let your friends figure out their lives, regardless of the advice you give them, it's up to them to take your advice, at the end of the day it's their life, not yours. "

"I do understand that, but you should have seen the way he beat her up, I don't know why she would take a man back who did that to her."

"Now, you don't know for sure that she took him back, right?"

"No, I don't but she has been missing in action and acting very secretive, even her mother said it."

"I can understand you guys caring for her, but you have to let her figure this out herself, you can only be there for her when she needs you, that's all I can say, she's your friend and you know her better than me."

"I get what you are saying but damn I just wish there was something I could do or say."

"I believe you've done all you can, now it's up to her and her decisions, if she wants to deal with this man, or should I say coward, who beats her up and if she decides to take him back or not."

"You said it right, he's a damn coward, I know what you are telling me is right, but I just, I just don't know."

"Well, come here and let me take your mind off that, at least temporarily, things will work themselves out, I guarantee."

"I pray you are right; I am glad I have you to talk to," I said as I went over, and sat on James's lap.

"You have me, and I have you, and I am glad you chose to confide in me, now am I staying the night or what, it has gotten late and dark outside." "If you want to, I will get you a towel, but did you bring any clothes?"

"Actually, I did, they are in my gym bag, I was on my way to the gym when you called me.

"Okay, go and get them and I will run your bath water." "Okay, sounds good." James went to his car to get his things and I went to run him some water. I started having flashbacks of him making love to me as I lathered up his water in the tub.

When he came back in, his bath water was just about ready. "Come up here, baby, I am up here."

"Okay, I am coming, I got my things," James said as he made his way upstairs. "Your water is ready, here's your towel, and your washcloth," I said as I headed out of the bathroom. "Hold up, where are you going, aren't you going to take one with me?" "I didn't know if you wanted me to." "Woman, get naked and get on in here." "But I already took a shower." "So, what, get in here with me." "Okay, since you put it like that, all demanding." "Ha, ha, whatever, you know you want to get in here with me." I didn't say I didn't, just a little surprised." I said as I started taking off my clothes. We both got into the tub and James held me as I sat in front. The water and his body felt so good, all I could do was relax and enjoy the moment. It felt great!

CHAPTER ELEVEN

Just To Say I Got A Man

After a night of great sex with James, it was time to get up for work. James left right before I got dressed. I was starting to feel alive again and I could see the glow upon me as I finished putting on my clothes. I made a cup of coffee and then I was out the door on my way to work.

I stopped at a red light and just as I was about to pull off, my phone rang. "Damn, who's calling me this early?" I said to myself. It was my Dad calling me and he said, "Hello," "Dad, how are you, are you okay?" "Good morning, of course, I am okay, why, what's going on?" "Nothing are you here in town?" "No, I am at home in California, why do I need to be there?" "No, Dad, I was only asking because you are calling, me so early and I know we are at least three hours ahead in the time zone." "Yeah, I know, I was just thinking about you." "Any reason why, and why this early?" "You know your sister called me and said you were seeing a new guy?" "That stank, ooh, she talks too much." "Ha, ha, calm down, she said you met a good guy, I was only thinking about that last punk you were with, I hope he's nothing like that." "No way Dad, he's a good man, so far, and his name is James." "James. Huh, so far, huh, okay, I am just checking like a father is supposed to do." "No need to worry Dad, I am okay." "Okay then, I know you have to go to work, so just keep in touch with me, I should be coming back to visit on the 4th of July." "Okay Dad, sounds good, I love you." "I love you too, bye, talk to you later," Dad said as he hung up the phone.

I love my Dad very much. That phone call brought one tear to my eye. I know he cares about me, and I appreciate him for that, but on the other hand, my sister Monique talks too damn much.

I finally made it to work and the same as the day before, all the girls met in the parking lot except Amanda. "Have you girls talked to Amanda," I asked. "No, I haven't," Sylvia said. "April, there is something I have to tell y'all," Rochelle said with hesitance. "What?" Sylvia asked. "Yes, what, what's going on?" I asked. "Well, Amanda called me last week and told me she was going to give her crazy ass ex another chance." "What the hell, what?" Sylvia yelled. "Hell no, he almost killed her girl, Rochelle why didn't you tell me this shit last week?" "You know how Amanda is, plus she made me promise that I wouldn't tell you, April." "Because she knows, I wouldn't go for that shit, ooh, I am so pissed off at her, and Rochelle, you aren't off the damn hook either." "What, what did I do, I was only carrying out her wishes," Rochelle said.

I was so upset that I just walked away. "Wait, don't be mad at me," Rochelle said. "You should have told us, girl," Sylvia said. "But she made me promise," Rochelle said as I kept on walking.

I immediately called Amanda, but there was no answer. I called several more times and still nothing. I left about five messages for her to call me back. The whole morning, I was worried because she hadn't called me back.

By lunchtime, the girls and I met up. "Rochelle, have you gotten in touch with Amanda yet, because she isn't answering my calls?" I asked. "No, I have been calling her also, but nothing," Rochelle said in a sad tone. "I am not going to lie, I don't feel right about this, because Amanda would at least answer the phone, this isn't like her," Sylvia said.

All day we tried to contact Amanda, but she never answered. By the end of the day, we left her about thirty messages combined. "Do you think we should go by her house?" Sylvia asked as we walked out into the parking lot. "I know right, I was thinking the same thing, but maybe we shouldn't do that." I said, "I am with you, April, you know how private Amanda tries to be, maybe she has something going on," Rochelle said. "I didn't know," Sylvia said. "Maybe you are right, but if she doesn't answer by sometime tonight, I am going to take my ass over her house with or without y'all. Okay?" I said as I got into my car and pulled off. I called about five more times before I made it home.

As soon as I walked into the house, James called me. "Hey April, are you coming to class this evening?" "Oh hey, James, I am sorry I didn't call you today, I probably won't be in class this evening because I have a lot on my mind." "Are you okay, what's going on, you sound disgruntled?" "I am worried about my friend Amanda." "Isn't she the friend who got attacked by her man and ended up in the hospital?" "Yes, that's her, and I am afraid that she got back with that crazy muthafucka." "Why do you think that?" "Well, you know my friend, Rochelle, I was telling you about?" "Yes, I think so, she's the tall one in white in the picture with you on your nightstand, right?" "Yes, she told me that Amanda did decide to give that crazy man another chance." "She did what, is she crazy?" "She must be, I wish I had known, I would have said or done something." "Remember what I told you before, they are grown and sometimes you have to stay out of grown folks' mess, but I know how caring you are and that is your friend." "Yes, she is my friend, and I can't stand back and watch her waste her life on someone who doesn't really care about her, and all he does is hurt her, I mean come on now, just so she can say she got a man, it's not worth it." "Yeah, you are right." "I have been calling her all day and no answer and now I am getting worried." "Wow, she hasn't answered all day?" "Nope, and that's not like her." "Why don't you go over to her house?" "I was just thinking about that, and I probably will after I get out of the shower." "Well, okay then, go check on her, and keep me posted." "I will, I will talk to you later, baby, bye." "Okay, bye," James said we hung up.

I called Amanda one more time before I got into the shower and still no answer. I was really worried at this point because as far as I knew, nobody had heard from her.

I showered and threw on my black workout leggings, and my black and grey stretch workout top, and I put on my tennis shoes. Just as I was about to grab my house keys and walk out the door, my phone rang.

I looked down and I could see it was Amanda's mother, Ms. Brooks, calling me. I was hoping she had some good news and that she had heard from Amanda, but as soon as I answered, all I heard was her yelling, screaming, and crying.

"Ms. Brooks, calm down, calm down, what's wrong?" I yelled in panic. "Ahhh, no. no. no, he killed my baby." She screamed; The terror immediately hit my soul. "What, what, who, who killed who?" I asked as I panted. "He killed her, he killed her, that muthafucka, I will kill him, that man, she didn't have to take him back, ah, no, God, not my baby, no, no, no." She yelled and screamed.

"Not, Amanda, tell me no. please tell me to know." I screamed as the tears came running down my face.

"Yes, yes, they found her dead in her house with two bullet wounds to the head and she was beaten badly with a couple of broken ribs, oh no, I am going to kill that bitch."

"No, tell me this isn't so, where is he, did they arrest him, oh my God this can't be happening, Ms. Brooks are you there?" I asked as I could hear people trying to help Ms. Brooks breathe.

"Ms. Brooks, Ms. Brooks," I called out repeatedly.

"He killed her, he took my baby, oh, no, the police are looking for him, now, please come."

"I am on my way Ms. Brooks, where are you?"

"I am over at Amanda's house, they are about to take her body, please hurry." She said as her voice rose to a pitch higher than her own. I could tell she was crying and stuttering and spitting up, she was slurring her words.

At that moment, I felt so damn helpless, hurt, and confused. I didn't waste any time after that, I just hopped in my car and called the girls. They were crying up a storm, especially Rochelle. I believe guilt had set in because she felt she should've said something.

I told her it wasn't her fault, but she kept crying and crying as we talked on the phone. I made it to Amanda's house in about thirty-five minutes her family cars were there and so were the police and the paramedics. I could see the pain on everybody's faces as I got out of my car. The girls pulled up just as I was approaching the house. We all got out of our cars, and we hugged each other tightly as the paramedics hoisted Amanda's covered body into the ambulance.

Ms. Brooks saw me, and she ran into my arms. We both started crying and asking why. Rochelle and Sylvia came behind us and hugged us and the tears just started rolling down our faces, it was one of the saddest moments of my life, I kept trying to hold Ms. Brooks up as she cried and asked why this happened over and over again. I don't have the answers for her, I only cried and held on to her. My heart pounded in my chest; I was in utter disbelief.

CHARLES LEE ROBINSON JR.

As soon as the paramedics closed the door of the ambulance, Ms. Brooks went into a frenzy. "No, no, don't take her, my baby, Amanda, no, why, why, why God, no, ah, ah, Lord no, please, don't take her, don't you take my baby." She screamed out in a horrifying screech. All we could do was hold her, comfort her, and cry as if we were all in shock.

"The police just called, and they said they captured his ass." Amanda's cousin Gloria said. "That's good they got that muthafucka, I am going to kill him myself." Amanda's cousin Marvin said.

"They got him, Ms. Brooks," I said as we all picked her up and took her into the house. We were all shocked and relieved that he was captured but there was a deep wound in our hearts, and it was filled with emptiness and pain. Why did she take him back?

The day of Amanda's funeral was so emotional. I stood next to the girls and James was at my side. We were all dressed in black, and everybody had tears in their eyes. We were all praying in disbelief that our loved one was now about to be buried.

I stood there and I prayed to God. I prayed for my friend, and I prayed for Ms. Brooks to have strength. A beautiful woman lost her life only to just say she got a man. He wasn't a man at all. No man would kill such a beautiful soul, this way. I hope he rots in jail. As we said our prayer and placed roses on her coffin, they lowered it. Ms. Brooks started crying and screaming again. "No, don't take her, don't go, Amanda, I love you, please don't take her, Lord get her out of there," She yelled as everyone held her and tried to calm her down. That was awful to watch. My heart just dropped, and I cried as I had never cried before. Weeks later after Amanda was buried, Rochelle came to me and she said, "I kicked Bernard out of my house finally, the papers came through and I evicted his ass. "That's wonderful Rochelle, you deserve better," I said. "I know I do; I sure miss Amanda." She said. "I do too, her laugh, her smile, and her crazy sense of humor, she didn't deserve that." "I know, I know, so I saw you and you knew man, how is that going?" "It's going, you know, one day at a time," I said. "Sylvia called me and told me that she broke it off with her man and her other friend." "Huh, what other friend?" "Never mind, you have to ask her." "Okay, I will, well good luck." She said. "And the same to you, I love you, girl," I said as we hugged.

I believe the day we lost Amanda brought light into our eyes; I mean the realization of what can happen if you are with the wrong person. It's okay to be alone sometimes. It doesn't make you half a woman just because you don't have a man and another woman does, just live the life, God has for you.

I pray this relationship with James works out but only God knows. I can tell you this if he ever starts acting up, I won't hesitate to let his ass go, and I am not playing. Amanda shouldn't have to die just because she wanted half a man in her life.

I hope this wakes all of you up and realizes your self-worth, once you know that, you won't ever accept anything less than what you deserve.

"April, are you ready to go?" "Yes, I will be right there James," I said as I got in his car and headed to dinner. "Oh my, you look beautiful April." He said. "And, you, you are very handsome," I said as James leaned over to give me a gentle and passionate kiss.

Although my heart was sad, joy crept into my heart as I had good thoughts about Amanda and all the good times we had. I will miss my girl, and I pray good times are ahead for James and me, but only time will tell. I know my boundaries and I know what I will accept, and with that being said I will never stay with a man, just to say I got a man. "Now let's enjoy this dinner."

THE END!!!

CHARLES LEE ROBINSON JR.

LOVE DOESN'T HAVE A NAME

PROLOGUE

"Oh my God, yes this is good, keep giving it to me Daddy." "Do you like that baby?" "Oh yes, Mozelle, give me more, give me, ah, ah," Danielle said. Just as she released her climax, I was just about to, and then I heard a loud knocking at the door. The voice was very deep and it was thunderous. "Danielle, I know your home, who in the hell do you have in this house?"

Danielle jumped up out of the bed like a cat can land on his feet every time you toss him from an upside-down position. I jumped up fast and I started getting dressed as fast as I could. The only thing wrong was, my clothes didn't agree with me. I had one leg in my pants, my shirt was inside out, and I couldn't find my other sock. "I thought you said you don't have a man?" "He's not my man, he's my ex and he won't leave me alone," Danielle whispered. "Well, if he's not your man then why are you whispering?" Danielle was speechless. The knock at the door got louder along with some loud kicks to the door. "Danielle if you have another man in this house, I am killing you and him." "Oh shit, get dressed, get dressed." "I am trying to but, damn, I can't believe this shit, Danielle," I said. "It's not my fault, damn this man is crazy." "Oh, now you tell me, Danielle." I finally got my things together and my clothes on. I went by the front window in her bedroom and I stood to the side while trying to see Danielle's ex. He was a huge man. He looked like he was six-two and close to 300 lbs. All I could think was, *damn Mozelle look what you've got yourself in this time.*

CHAPTER ONE

This Is Some Mess

As I stared out her window, I watched his every move. He started pacing back and forth and every once in a while, he would kick or hit the door extremely hard. "What's this guy, or you're ex's name, with his big ass?" "His name is Marvin but his street name is Big Crazy M." "What the hell, what type of name is that?" "Never mind, never mind, how in the hell do I get out of here?" "There's only one way to get out here, which is the front door."

My heart dropped to the floor like a pebble being thrown off the Empire State Building and killing a civilian once it hit them in the head. I paced back and forth. "We got to think, we got to think," I said as I rubbed my sweaty forehead. "I don't know what we can do Mozelle." "Ah, the wrong answer, you better think of something quick," I said anxiously. "I got an idea." "What's your idea?" "I will go to the back of the house, yell his name, and make him think I am trying to escape back there." I paced back and forth and then I went back to the window while watching Big Crazy M walk back and forth cursing and talking to himself. No matter what, he wasn't leaving. I thought long and hard and then I said, "Okay it's worth a try."

Danielle ran up to me and she tried to kiss me, I softly mugged her face. I don't hit women, but she's trying to get me killed and then wants a kiss. No way! So, Danielle tiptoed to the other room, the way she was tip-toeing looked like she had sharp tacks on her floors. She screamed through that back window and just like she said Big Crazy M fell for it. As soon as he moved from in front of the house I dashed out.

As I was running to my car, I could see him running back towards the front and he said, "You think you slick." I didn't look back, I just hopped in my BMW and I was gone. I looked back once and that was it. All I could think of was why this girl didn't tell me she had a crazy ass ex by the name of Big Crazy? That name alone would've scared the hell out of my dick. He probably would've remained limp for a long, long time, I mean damn. I drove to the nearest bar because, after this wild shit, I needed a drink. I saw club Roxie open, so I decided to stop there. It was a small bar near my house.

We called it a little hole in the wall. There's something about them little holes in the walls. They play the best music and they keep the sexiest women in them. I walked in and headed straight to the bar which was on my left. I could see the dartboard in the back and tables against the left wall. The lights were dim with red and black color coordination going on. There were sexy women everywhere. I got my drink and I went and sat at the table. I only wanted one drink and I was heading home. At least that was the plan. Soon as I was about to leave three beautiful women walked in with hourglass-figured shapes.

The short one with the long hair, white pants, and tan hauteur top winked her eye at me and then I sat my happy ass back down. I watched them go to the bar. I could hear everyone snickering in the bar about the three ladies.

The young lady got brave and had the bartender send me a drink. I held my glass up to her to thank her and then she walked over to my table. She said her name was Andrea. We talked and laughed and then we exchanged numbers. I told her I was leaving. We hugged and then I watched her big ass walk back over to her friends. I hadn't noticed that arch in her back until then. That ass was so big, you could sit a plate and a cup of water on it, "Oh my."

CHAPTER TWO

Look at What You've Done Now

I went home that night and I got myself in the shower. I smelled like VJ (vagina) all night. As soon as I got out of the shower, Andrea called me. We talked on the phone all night. It's been a long time since I've been on the phone with a woman like that. Andrea asked me to come over to her house the next night. I agreed, I thought what could it hurt.

The next day came, and I put on some nice clothes. Fitted grey slacks, a black belt, and a white button-up shirt with a black Movado watch. I pulled out my Izzy cologne. *I looked handsome if I do say so myself*, I thought. I drove up and down West Santos Drive, which is on the Westside of Rochester, New Work. I called Andrea because I couldn't see the houses well. She said she would come outside so I could see her. From afar I could see an arm waving with a white shirt. It was Andrea so I stopped, and she showed me where to park. I got out of the car, and we went into the house. Soon as I sat down Andrea started giving me compliments. I thanked her. She kept getting and getting things out of the kitchen like grapes, and cheese squares, and then she brought out some wine. I sat back and relaxed with my legs wide open and I started wagging them back and forth.

We sipped our wine, and we ate cheese and grapes. I felt so relaxed and the next thing I knew Andrea was zipping down my zipper and pulling down my pants. I had a look of surprise on my face until she pulled out all that dick. "Oh my, where do you plan to put all this?"

She held it in her hands and before I could say anything, she engulfed it. I was paralyzed as she kissed, and she sucked on it. She held it as if it was her first child. I started pulling all my clothes off wildly. Then she took her clothes off. I quickly turned her around so I could see all that ass.

CHARLES LEE ROBINSON JR.

The spread on her looked like a 50-inch screen TV. I pulled out my protection and started pounding her with hard strikes and she moaned loudly. Our bodies were mixing well. We started sweating, so our bodies became slippery. I counted one hundred back shots in my head.

The counting in my mind helped my stamina. I laid her on the floor and moaned as I drove in and out of her like a drive-through. The passion was unreal. "Give it to me daddy, yes, yes, oh it feels so good." Then she stuck her nails deep into my chest and then my back. I moved her hands because man, that shit hurts. I kept pounding and pounding until we both came. She jumped up fast and ran to the shower. After her shower, I was half dressed and Andrea brought out a washcloth for me with soap on it. I washed myself up. Then Andrea told me I had to leave. I looked at her and said, "Are you serious?" "Yes, I am very serious; you have to leave because my husband gets off work in ten minutes." "What the fuck, why didn't you tell me, that you were married?" I asked while still in shock. "You never asked me, now I got what I wanted now go, plus love doesn't have a name." "What is that supposed to mean?" "Man, just go, before my husband gets here and he kills both of our asses." I shook my head and I felt like a cheap whore, I felt worse than a cheap Lyell Avenue whore. Andrea used me. I got my things together and I looked down at my dick and I said," look at what you've done now."

CHAPTER THREE

I Can't Believe This Here

I was hurt that night that Andrea pulled that mess on me. I wasn't going to stop looking for that love I was searching for. I had to find it. I was all in my thoughts as I lay in my bed. Why can't I find a good woman? What am I doing wrong? I got lost in my thoughts so once again I needed a drink. I found a little bar called Zone Out.

They zone out in here, I tell you. You can smell weed everywhere you walk. I swear even security was smoking. I saw a couple in the corner smoking on a bong. I started getting a contact with the smoke so I hurried and left.

As soon as I got out the door, I saw a tall young lady outside sniffling and crying. I walked up to her because she was all alone. She had long straight shoulder-length brown hair, nice tight jeans, and a white shirt with her arms showing and her legs spread apart. I asked, "Are you, ok Miss?" "No, I am not okay." "May I ask you what the problem is?" "This guy I was talking to just left me here." "He left you; he did what, and why?" "I don't know, he said I was crazy." "That's nonsense, why would he call you that?" She shrugged her shoulders. "You look pretty sane to me." "I don't know, listen can you please give me a ride home?" I looked her up and down." You want me to take you home, are you sure, what will your man say?" "I don't have a man, he wasn't my man, we were just hanging out and having a good time, you know here and there?" "Here and there, what does that mean, were you two sleeping together?" "Sometimes we did, but not all the time." "I had a very bad gut feeling about this. "Where do you live?" "I live in Charlotte near Ontario Beach." Damn, that's far." "Please sir, and what is your name?" "My name is Mozelle, well, it's Joeb Mozelle but, everyone calls me Mozelle." "Mozelle please take me home I promise to pay you." "Hold up, I don't know your name." "My name is Diana." I thought for a minute or two. I decided to take her home even though my gut feelings were telling me not to. After close to an hour's drive, we made it to her house. She talked me half to death along the way.

The house was white, and it looked mysterious because it sat alone. "Do you want to come in, I live alone." "Who stays here with you Diana?" "No one I live here alone, come on please, come on in." "What will it hurt; okay I will come in for a while. I walked in and I almost stumbled and then Diana turned on the lights. The house was small but very cozy.

She had old-fashioned furniture, but it looked expensive. I sat down on her sofa." Do you want something to drink?" "Sure, what do you have?" "I have Cognac, white wine, OJ, and water." "I already had something to drink, so water is good." Diana went and got a bottle of water for me. "I am going in the room to get into something comfortable, you can come in my room. I had a look on my face as if to say, *Oh boy!* I sat on Diana's bed, and she began taking off all her clothes in front of me. Her body was nice, I stared at her up and down. She turned around and she came towards me with no clothes on. I was in a state of shock because this was not the plan. She started stroking and rubbing my dick. "Oh wow! it's huge." It began to rise. She shoved me back on the bed so hard, I thought I was in a shoving match.

CHARLES LEE ROBINSON JR.

My head hit the bed and the next thing I knew she was kissing and sucking on me. I started breathing heavily. She was so good at the head job that I almost came quickly. No one had ever made me get to that point so fast. I pushed her off me to get a breather, but she got right back on it. I pushed off again. "Give me some of this dick; I want it now, now," Diana said.

Her whole demeanor changed and not for the best. "Sex me Dammit; Sex me, put this big dick in me now. I started getting worried because she sounded like the girl from the exorcist. So, I did what she said. I pulled out my big dick and tried to put it in. It wouldn't fit. I tried and I tried. Diana went to get lubricant. We tried again and I only could penetrate with the head of my dick. She started cursing me out badly. "Muthafucka, give me some of that dick now. I jumped up and I went to grab my clothes.

Diana started grabbing me and cursing loudly. I was worried because I didn't want the police to come and think I was trying to rape this crazy lady. I tried to put on my pants but they got stuck on my ankles. She started getting crazier by the second. She started hitting me. I finally got away and I ran out the door with my pants and my underwear stuck on my ankles. I tripped as I got to my car. I saw Diana trying to run toward my car with a shoe with a long heel on it. She shot it at my car, I jumped in and I pulled off fast and almost had an accident. I made it home and I lay in my bed still sweating up a storm and I said, *I can't believe this here.* After that day I decided that

I would stay alone and I wouldn't just jump into bed with a woman I don't know well. That's the reason those relationships weren't going anywhere. Next time I will be more cautious and I will get to know a person first. Good sex isn't always good sex. As Andrea said, Love Doesn't Have a name.

THE END!!!

CHARLES LEE ROBINSON JR.

FRIENDS WITH BENEFITS

PROLOGUE

"Ahhh, yes, daddy, ahhhh, yes, yes, lick it, ahhhhh." "Do you like that baby?" "Yes, yes, I do daddy." Oh, this right here is my friend Donny, just look at him slurping all on my PUSSY. I love the way he licks and kisses between my legs. Then I tremble and I cum. Well, that's all Donny is good for he's 6'2 and has a small dick. I know what you're saying, "Oh no, not a small dick." "Unfortunately, it's true.

All of this, and this man wasn't blessed in that area, but he does have a wicked tongue. "Good night, Donny." "Good night, will I see you again?" He asked as he made it to his car. "I hope not," I whispered. "What, what did you say Valencia?" "Oh nothing, drive carefully."

As soon as he drove off, I felt relieved. I hate a man who ain't good for nothing but eating my PUSSY. I know, I know, it might sound cruel, but I need, and I want a stallion, a man who can last all night long, and put me in one hundred positions. You heard right, even if there ain't one hundred, make some up. Plus, he must have length and girth, I like getting my PUSSY eaten, but I need some insertion. I'm glad he's gone. I went straight to the closet, pulled out my dildo, and I went to work. After that, I still want the real thing. I went, showered, and took my behind to sleep; pissed off.

CHAPTER ONE

I Went Out With The Girls

After messing around with Donny, I was bored. I had to let him go. He kept calling me and leaving messages. Finally, I answered the phone and I said, "Donny, I can't see you anymore, because I'm in a relationship now." This idiot said, "Okay, can I still eat it?" I hung up on his ear. *Meet Mr. Click little man*, I thought to myself. Later that week I went out with a few of my girlfriends. We were all having a good time and getting drunk. Guys kept coming up to our table and offering drinks. My friend Tamara kept accepting the drinks.

My friend Rachael was right along with her. "All right if you keep accepting drinks, these men are going to want something in return," I said. "Only thing these idiots can get, is a taste," Tamara said while she started twirling her ass.

Then she and Rachael gave each other a high five. "Nobody worried about these damn idiots; if they want to spend their money on us, then let them," Rachael said. "You girls are too much, but you will learn, anyway, I have to go to the ladies' room, you girls watch my drink please." "Okay girl, go with your weak bladder ass," Tamara said. "Whatever, whatever," I said as I stood up and pulled my short skirt down.

The bar was crowded and I had to wait in line to get into the ladies' room. I had to cross my legs, and I was shaking, just to keep from pissing on myself. Finally, I made it to the restroom; and just in time. I felt so much relief after that. I stood in the restroom looking in the mirror, making sure my makeup was still correct, then I washed my hands. Some of the girls didn't wash their hands t

CHARLES LEE ROBINSON JR.

CHAPTER TWO

It Went Down

I headed back toward where my friends were sitting, and then I felt a hand grab my arm. I usually curse a person out for grabbing my arm, but just when I was going to say something, my eyes locked with the sexiest man in the room. Oh, my God, this brother was fine and chocolate and he smelled so good, I damned near fainted. "Excuse me, may I ask your name?"

For a moment I forgot my own damn name. "My name is uh, my name is uh, oh my name is Valencia, sorry, I think I've had too many drinks." "What's your name if you don't mind me asking?" "My name is Steven, by the way, that's okay, are you single?" "Yes, I am very single, are you, and don't lie." "Valencia, I am very single." "Well, that's good, nice to meet you Steven, but I have to get back to my friends." Look at me, trying not to let him know that I think he is so fine. "Can we exchange numbers or something?" "Yes, we can." I looked at Steven up and down and all I could think about was him and his manhood. Yes, I did, I looked at his crouch, fine as he is, that brother better be packing, that's all I'm saying. We exchanged numbers. Then I heard a big commotion as I looked for the table we were sitting at.

All I saw were shoes and bottles flying. I couldn't see who was fighting until, I heard Rachael say, "Kick his ass girl, whoop his ass, oh you want some too?" Rachael said. The security guard quickly rushed in. Those damn wild girls got into a fight with the same guys who were buying their drinks. Security made us leave. "What the hell happen Tamara?" I asked. "That idiot brought my drink and then he groped on my breast." "No, he didn't." "Yes, he did," Rachael said. "So, what happened then?" "What do you mean what happened, I kicked his ass, I bet he won't touch another woman like that." "I told you two, to stop accepting drinks from those guys, but you didn't want to listen to me." "Yes, you said it, now I know." "What took you so long in the restroom, anyway, were you in the fixing of your tampon?" Tamara asked. "Hell no, nasty ass." "I met this fine brother near the restroom, his name is Steven." "Steven, what?" Rachael asked." "I didn't ask his last name." "Your ass is crazy, you better ask their last name next time, mess around and be a cousin." They both laughed. "Damn, I can't leave you for one second before shoes start flying everywhere," I said. "Girl, I got his ass good too, he thought it was funny until that left hook caught his jaw," Tamara said. "Girl it was a right hook, with your drunken ass," Rachael said. We laughed. I took those crazy fools home and I headed home myself.

As I was pulling up to my driveway, my phone rang. I answered the phone in my cute sexy voice. "Hello, who is this?" "Hey lady, this is Steven, what are you doing?" "Oh, Hi Steven, I just got home, what are you doing?" "I am out with my friends having a bite to eat." "Well, I am about to shower and go to sleep." "Okay, I don't want to keep you from your beauty sleep." "Thank you, give me a call tomorrow afternoon." "That sounds like a plan." We hung up the phone. *Damn, he sounds good as hell on the phone,* I said to myself. I couldn't stop thinking about how good Steven looked. I made it in the house. I showered and still had him on my mind. His cologne smelled so good. I could still smell it as if he were here with me. I climbed my way into bed after my shower. I started fantasizing about Steven. It felt weird because I just met him. I was horny, I don't know, I just kept having these freaky thoughts. I fell asleep thinking about him. *Damn, what a night.*

CHAPTER THREE

He Came Over

After I got out of bed the next morning, I made breakfast and did some laundry, and at about 3 p.m. I received a call from Steven. "Hey lady, what are you doing?" "Hello Steven, I am doing laundry, and you?" "I was just watching TV, so do you have any plans this evening?" "No, I plan on staying home today; I think I have a little hangover." I giggled. "Where do you live?" "I live in the Southside of the City; do you know where Riverview Drive is?" "I think I know where that is, is there a Seven-Eleven near there, close to the railroad tracks?" "Yes, that's it." "Would you like some company?" "Sure, why not, come to 45116 Riverview, it's a little white house, you can't miss it." "Okay, what time should I come?" "You can come about 7 p.m., by then, I'll be finished with all my chores." When we finally hung up the phone, I thought to myself, *damn what am I doing? I don't even know this guy. I believe my PUSSY was speaking for me,* I thought as I giggled. I had to call my girls after that. I called Rachael first. "Hello Rachael, what are you doing?" "I am trying to get over this hangover?" "How are you trying to do that?" "By drinking more liquor." "Your ass is crazy, but guess what?" "What?" is your ass still drunk too?" "No, I'm okay now, but remember that guy I told you I met last night?" "Yeah, I vaguely remember why?" "He called and he's coming over this evening?"

"Damn your ass is fast and easy too, girl you are whore?" "Really Rachael, did I say that when you just met that guy named Eric, and you gave him head on the first date?" "Oh, girl that was different." "Different, actually that was worse, but you're still my girl, just don't let me drink after you." "Whatever, with your fast ass, go ahead girl, and get yourself some, you might feel it in your spirit, and you know that calmness you get when you get good sex?" "Ha, ha, ha, well I haven't felt that in a long time, as a matter of a fact never." "This might be the one, you never know." "You're funny." "You won't think it's funny when he has your ass walking bowlegged." "That won't ever happen, bye girl." I hurried up and hung up the phone on that crazy girl. Then I called Tamara. "Hello Tamara, what are you doing?" "Nothing, girl, I am still in bed, my hands are sore." "Sore, ha, ha, that's what you get for hitting that man." "Girl, be quiet, he deserved it." "I am not trying to amp you up girl, but guess what?" "What?" "Do you remember that guy, I told you I met last night?" "The one you were so busy with while Tamara and I were kicking ass?" "Whatever girl, shoot I had to piss, I didn't tell you to turn into Rhonda Rouse." "I whoop that ass though, didn't I?" "Anyway, do you remember?" "I slightly remember, yes, why?" "I invited him over this evening." "Damn girl you're easy, your ass must be horny, you always messing with that little dick Donny with the super tongue." "Tamara, why did you have to go there?" "I went there because you're the one who told me about it." "Yeah, I did and that's all he's good for, but damn he licks a plate clean." "Ok, now I need a human dishwasher too." We both laughed.

"Okay girl whatever you do, just make sure he uses protection." "Okay, let me go get cleaned up before he comes." "Valencia, guess what?" "What Tamara?" "You are a whore." Before I could hang up, and respond, I heard Tamara laughing as she hung up in my ear. I have some crazy ass friends. Tamara can't talk though, she had sex with one leg Benny on the first night, and she had the nerve to ride him in his wheelchair. I laughed, now that was ewwwwe nasty, ha, ha, ha. Nasty ass!

CHAPTER FOUR

He Gave Me Some Good Dick

After talking to my crazy friends and getting myself together, Steven showed up at 7 p.m. He was looking very nice in his red and white. He was wearing red pants, a white button-up shirt, and a pair of red loafers. He looked delicious. Oops, I meant good, haha. I had to laugh about that. "Hey Steven, come in and have a seat." "Thank you, so what were you doing?" "Nothing at all just resting, would you like a glass of wine?" "Yes, sure, what kind do you have?" "I only drink red wine; I love the sweet ones." "That's good, I only drink those too, I hate that strong dry kind, they are bitter. "I know, I hate those too. I went and brought out our glasses of wine. We both got tipsy. Like a naughty little girl, I invited Steven into my bedroom.

We sat on the edge of my bed just talking at first. Then I went and turned on some music. Next, I lit the two big, scented candles I had on my dresser. I love that beautiful aroma. Then Steven and I started kissing passionately. The next thing I knew, we were both out of our clothes. *Steven slowly laid me in bed. He was so gentle with his hands and caresses. I closed my eyes, and I clinched the sheets as I felt his hot tongue run over the surface of my body, my PUSSY started to get hotter. I moaned loudly as he grazed my PUSSY with his tongue and lips. I started breathing heavily. Then I felt this hot wet cream fall down my leg, my legs trembled as I begin to cum. I thought to myself, he made me cum already, and he hasn't even penetrated me. He held my ass in both hands as I rose off the bed, I moaned and I groaned. "Oh, ahhhh, ohhh, ahhhh, baby," I said as my spirit was filled with passion. It was a passion I'd never felt before, the passion I only dreamed of. I couldn't believe this was happening to me. I never trembled like this. Then Steven put on the protection. He slowly opened my legs, and a sigh of relief came across my face, as I felt a huge insertion. "Oh, my God, Oh Jesus." "I called out the two names, I shouldn't have at the time, but I've been needing and wanting this feeling for a long time. "Ahhh, ahhhh, oooh, ooh ah, ah." I couldn't stop cumming. They were coming back-to-back. Steven was so far up in me; that I could feel him touching places I didn't know existed. I was on cloud nine, or cloud nineteen, but one thing I certainly knew was, I was no longer on earth. He put my legs high up in the air, and he held both of my ankles and made them form a triangle, then he drove into my sugar walls. Long strokes, one after another. It was like he was manipulating my PUSSY. I trembled so much until I lost control of my extremities. My body was all his. Then as I came harder than I ever had before, a small tear came out of my eye. "Baby, what's wrong are you, all right?" "Yes, baby, that was just a tear of joy, I thank you." Then Steven's strokes got tense and fast. Next, he roared as if he were the King of the jungle, and his body began to tremble, and then it came to an abrupt stop. "Did you cum, Daddy?" "Yes, I did, yes, I did." Steven lay on the side of me, and he held me tight. We both went to sleep.*

I woke up hours later and I couldn't believe what had happened. I lay there feeling tranquil, and my spirit felt fulfilled like a dream, which became a reality. I felt that from this man, and only him, I felt tranquility in my spirit. For the very first time in my life. Now I wondered, where will we go from here?

CHAPTER FIVE

Round Two In The Shower

Steven woke up the next morning. He looked at me and he smiled. I smiled back at him. "What just happened last night, was I dreaming?" "I don't think it was a dream, love." "Wow! That was great and so intense, I want some more." "If you want more, then I want some more too." "Great, let's shower and brush our teeth, damn that shit was good, I want more, no I need some more." "It's like that love?" "You just don't know." And we went and took a shower. The water trickled down our bodies and you could see the steam. *I grabbed the shower gel, and I began to wash every inch of his amazing body. I* stared at his chest, and I worked my way down. I grabbed his manhood and held that long juicy shaft in the air as I washed him thoroughly. Steven turned around and I washed his back. His little muscular ass started turning me on. When I finished washing him, my PUSSY was hot and wet. I trembled as I felt those juices flowing. "What's. wrong baby, I thought I saw you shaking." I smiled. "I think I came by just washing you and that sexy body." "Are those juices flowing right now?" I nodded my head up and down as if to say yes. Steven pushed me slowly to the back of the shower where little water could reach. Then he slid down and put his head between my legs. He started twirling his tongue on the outside of my PUSSY. He slowly put his tongue inside of me. I rose to my tippy toes, and then I gasped for air, "Ahhhh." My eyes went up in my head. He slurped all my juices as they oozed down the inside of my legs. Oh, my goodness. Steven and his hot tongue worked their magic. Steven held my ass cheeks tight and then he smacked one gently. "Ohhh, baby, Oooooh, baby, ah, ah, ah." Whatever I was trying to say wouldn't come out. Then I heard him moan as he licked and sucked. "Baby let's get out of the shower for **Round Two**. He was game and so was I. This man is incredible.

CHAPTER SIX

He Fucked Me Well

Round Two *was inevitable, it had to go down,* I thought to myself as Steven, and I lay down on the bed naked and half-wet in some places. I could feel our wet flesh slip and slide as we embraced each other. I found myself falling to Steven's feet and he was at mine. *I rolled up on top of him and I sat my PUSSY on his soft lips and hot tongue. I played with his manhood with my tongue. At first, I teased him a little and then I yelped as his hot tongue let me know that it was time to stop playing. So, I engulfed his entire manhood as he continued to make my PUSSY wet. Passion filled my body, and my eyes became glazed as we enjoyed that beautiful number called 69. This is the kind of lovemaking that you only see in the movies, and I'd been waiting for this all my life.* "Ahhhh, ahhhh, ahhhh, Ooooh, ahhhh Oooooh! The noises I made and the way he made my PUSSY feel were out of this world. After I watched all my sweet juices flow down his mouth and *cheeks, I rose slowly so he could put on his protection. From there I lost control. As he inserted every inch of that beast inside of me, my body tensed up. I grabbed for the air, and I grabbed for any and everything that wasn't there. "Oh damn, Oh damn Ooooh Ooooh." I tried to hold it in and then Steven started talking softly. "You like this dick, don't you?" "You want this dick, don't you?" I answered wildly. "Yes, yes, oh hell yes, give it to me, give it to meeeeeee! I held on to the word me as if I were holding on for dear life. "Oh my, oh my, I'm about to cum." Damn, he fucked me well! I think I can fall in love with this nigga! Oowweee, he got my PUSSY pulsating. That dick was so good!*

CHAPTER SEVEN

I Had To Tell My Girls

After we both had our orgasms and washed off, we fell asleep. I was in La, La Land, you hear me? The next morning Steven had to leave. We kissed passionately at the front door and then I said, "I will see you, later, right?" "Sure, you will," he said and then leaned over, and kissed me on my cheek. I felt so weak after I closed the door. I wobbled back upstairs. I started looking for my phone.

At first, I couldn't find it. Pillows were thrown everywhere; the sheets looked like they had been twisted. We tore that damn bed up, you hear me. A big smile came across my face after having flashbacks. I found my phone under the bed, and then I thought, "How in the hell did my phone get way under there?" I giggled. First, I called Rachael. "Hey, Rachael, what are you doing?" "Nothing, I just started cooking breakfast, what's up with you girl, did you get some dick?" "Ha, ha, girl you're funny, by the way, yes, yes and that shit was good, good, good," I said as I pulled the phone away from my ear to look at it. "Say what, He served your ass huh?" "My girl finally got that PUSSY waxed." "Girl will you be quiet." No, your ass be quiet." "Whatever." "I can't believe what I am hearing today, you are always having bad luck with guys in bed, and now you sound like your ass in love already, that must have been Superman's dick." "Ha, ha, ha," "Rachael stops laughing at me." "Girl I'm laughing with you, does he have a big dick, never mind, never mind he probably does, because your ass is acting bubbly this morning." "That's right, damn that shit was the bomb, and I mean uh, uh, uh good, do you hear me?" "Yes, I hear you, girl, Oh shit." "What's wrong?" "Let me call you back Valencia; I'm burning my damn breakfast." "Okay, bye girl."

I hung up with Rachael and then called Tamara to tell her the good news. The phone rang for a while and then Tamara answered the phone. "Tamara, why do you sound out of breath?" "Hello, is this Valencia?" "Yes, girl what are you doing?" "Tamara whispered, "Girl I'm fucking the shit out of old man Joe." "Girl no you're not, he's almost fifteen years older than you." "I don't give a damn, shit his bank account is fifteen times bigger than mine, and a Bitch, got to do what a Bitch got to do, bye V." "Did this damn girl hang up on me?" "Her nasty ass is having sex with old man Joe, that damn girl has lost her mind. I guess I will tell her later.

The rest of the day my head was up in the clouds. I did all my chores until late that evening. Then I realized about 10 p.m. that night, I hadn't heard from Steven. I tried calling his phone but I didn't get an answer. I called a few more times, and then I still didn't get any answer. I went and showered and went to bed holding my pillows.

CHAPTER EIGHT

Where The Hell Is Steven

I called Steven all that week, but no answer. I tried not to get into my feelings, I didn't know him that well and we weren't at all serious. I know I had to suck that one up to the game. Deep down I was wishing he would at least answer the damn phone. Tamara called me after work.

The phone rang and I jumped and quickly answered it, I thought it was Steven. "Damn girl, what are you so hyped about, you're breathing on the phone like a dog hunching on your ass or something." "Tamara please, and you're over there sucking on an old man's grey-haired balls." "Whatever, don't hate." "Tamara no one is hating on you, as a matter of fact, an old lady with a cane doesn't hate on you and old man Joe." "Ha, ha, ha, he, he, that shit isn't funny, now why are you breathing hard Valencia?" "No reason girl, I just thought you were someone else." "You thought I was someone else?" "Someone like whom?" "Oh, and Rachael told me you got dicked down." "That damn girl can't hold water." "Nope. She sure can't, so who is this sweet dick, Willie?" "Huh?" "Huh hell girl, if you said huh, then your ass heard me." "His name is Steven which I was trying to tell you the other day." "So, someone finally tore that ass out of the frame huh?" "Girl will you be quiet." "Quiet hell, that's why your sprung ass is running to your phone breathing all heavy." "So where is this, Steven?" "I don't know." "What do you mean you don't know, don't tell me that fool got the PUSSY and then he disappeared." "Girl don't even trip, we didn't have any commitment." You just told on yourself, uh huh, he got the PUSSY, and you haven't heard from him." "It's not that serious, we just met, nothing serious." "Is this the same guy you met at the club?" "Yes, it's the same one." "Why did you ask me that Tamara?" "Well, if you can't get in contact with him by phone, then I bet you can find his ass where you met him, in the damn club." "Girl, I am not looking for that man." "You don't have to, because I am." "Say what, leave it alone Tamara." "I'm going to give you a chance to handle it because if I handle it, it might just get a little ugly." "Your ass is a fool." "Hmmm, wait until I tell Rachael this shit, he got the PUSSY and disappeared." "Why do you have to tell her, I thought it was going to be between you and me." "Valencia, when did we sign a contract between you and me?" I was speechless. "Anyway, get yourself dressed because we have a club to go to." "Girl."

The next thing I heard was a click of the phone. That girl hung up on me. I tried to call Steven again, but his phone just rang. "Damn Steven, where are you? I asked as I looked at the phone. I got up and I found some clothes to wear to the bar. I jumped in the shower and began to have visions of Steven making passionate love to me. I closed my eyes tightly. It felt so real; it felt like he was still here touching me and kissing me. I could feel his hot tongue sucking on my nipples.

Before I knew it, I was rubbing and caressing my PUSSY. I had to catch myself. Damn, what has this man done to me? I asked. I guess sometimes you must watch what you ask for. I had to get my exposure. I got out of the shower and dried off. I put on my clothes and headed out of the house to get in my car. Then Rachael called me. "Valencia, where are you?" 'I'm just getting into the car, where are you?" "I am with Tamara crazy ass, and yes she filled me in." "Damn, neither one of you guys can't hold water." "Nope, we sure can't." "What are you going to say when you see him?" I don't know girl."

CHAPTER NINE

We Got In The Club

The girls and I met in the parking lot of the club. "Hey, Valencia." "What's up, Rachael?" "Are you ready to go in?" "Yes, I am Tamara, please don't go in here and embarrass me." "Valencia, I came out to have a good time, I was just letting you know where he might be since this is where you guys met." Rachael had an evil grin on her face. "Not you Rachael." "What boo, boo, just go handle your business." I shook my head, and we headed inside the bar. "Hold up, hold up, a deep voice shouted out. "It was that big-ass security guy who saw Tamara fighting the other week. "Don't I know you, ladies?" "No, we never saw you before in our lives." "I gave Tamara a look as if to say, "With your lying ass."

The other security guard is named Mike, and I know him very well. He's another big brother, but he's working with a pinky finger, but he loves me to death. "Mike, can you get us in?' I whispered in his ear." "Yeah, I got you, hey they are all right man, let them in." We made our way inside and I gave Mike a wink. "His little dick ass." Tamara, will you be quiet?" I said. Rachael just laughed.

We went straight to the bar and ordered our drinks. I looked around the bar, but I didn't see Steven. We went and sat at our usual spot.

The bar's owner recognized us, and he walked over, and he said, I know who you are, now please no fighting tonight." "We won't, we won't, we promise," Tamara said. Then he walked away. "Did you hear him with his raspy ass voice?" "Tamara chill out, you're lucky he let us stay up in here." "No, he's lucky, that we're in this juke joint." We laughed.

CHAPTER TEN

I Talked To Steven

We started drinking and getting tipsy. Guys kept offering to buy us drinks, but this time the girls were politely turning them down. I was so proud of them. We hit the dance floor and danced and sang along with the songs. "My shoes are hurting me, girl, I need to sit down," Rachael said. "Nobody told your ass to come dancing with hooker shoes on." "Girl shut the hell up, these aren't hooker shoes, are they Valencia?" Damn, why did she put me in this?" "No girl, don't listen to her." "Shit, Valencia, is the one who named them that," Tamara said. "On that note, I have to use the restroom." "Girl, go ahead with that weak ass bladder." "You said that?" I hurried and went to the restroom.

As soon as I came out, I saw Steven in the corner talking to some chick. I waited with my arms folded until they finished. Steven saw me and he tried to hide, but I walked over and stood right next to him, and the girl he was talking with. The girl must have felt uncomfortable, and then she left. I believe she made the right decision. "So, why haven't I heard from you all week, Mister?" "I am sorry Valencia, I wanted to call, but I was afraid that I would fall in love with you." "Say what Steven, listen we didn't make any commitment, you could at least have called, and let me know how you were doing?" "I know I should've." "I know you probably don't rush into any relationship and neither do I, I just want some companionship here and there, and we don't have to get serious." "I guess I could've handled things better." "Yes, you could've and who in the hell was that skinny bitch you were just talking to?" "She's nobody, really?" "Yeah, I bet, she looks young, so you over here getting your R. Kelly on huh?" Steven started laughing. I kept a serious look on my face. "Listen, no hard feelings between us, I think you're a cool guy, even though you hit it like that and disappeared." "I apologize, baby." "No need for apologies, look, my girls want me to tell your ass off, but I'm not." "Thank you, oh you told them?" "No, they figured it out on their own, because I told them about you when I first met you, and when they asked if I'd seen you again, I had to tell the truth." "Steven, around my girls, I have to act like I'm mad at you and I hate your guts, but can you do me one favor?" "What's that Valencia?" "After the club comes by my house, I have something waiting there for you, and it's hot juicy, and wet." I smiled and Steven smiled also.

As I walked away, he said in a whisper, "Bet, I can do that." Yes, I did that, shit, that man got some good head and dick on him, I'm not going to pass that up, even if it's just for one more night. I went back and I finished having fun with my girls until the bar closed. We stood in the parking lot chatting. "I guess I was wrong Valencia, I thought your friend Steven would be here," Tamara said. "He must be locked up in jail or something," Rachael said. I didn't say a word. It wasn't their business anyway. All that ran through my mind was, I had to hurry home to get this good loving.

After we left, I ran into the house, jumped in the shower, and lotion up good. I poured a glass of wine and got ready for the night of my life. My PUSSY started pulsating, just thinking about Steven bringing that big package home to momma. *Yes, yes*, I thought to myself. Damn, I am so horny, and I am not ashamed. Finally, after a few sips of my wine, Steven was at my door. He called me as he pulled into my driveway, and I hurried to let him in. Now let this night begin. "Okay?"

CHAPTER ELEVEN

Friends With Benefits

When Steven came inside the house it was on. We started kissing all the way up the stairs. I wasn't wasting any time. Yawl might call me a hussy, but I don't care, if you got dick as good as this, you would get it too, now back to my business. I took off my clothes and Steven pulled off his. I turned my ass around and assumed the position. I put an arch in my back so I can take it all. I could hear Steven ripping open the condom wrapper.

Then I heard him say, oh shit." I turned slightly and said. "What's wrong Daddy?" "Oh, nothing I dropped the rubber so I'm getting another one." "Don't get scared now." Steven laughed and he put on another one."

Next thing you know I was moaning so loudly, his first strokes woke up my PUSSY, I could feel her get wetter and expand. He gave me long strokes from the back as he held my wide hips in his hands. I heard him moaning and groaning as he gave me a shot back, after back shot. "Oh Daddy, give it to me." "How does it feel baby." Ooh, ahhhh, Ooooh, damn that dick is so good and so big." "Oh, baby, oh, damn this PUSSY is good." "Get it Daddy it's all yours."

Then Steven flipped me like a rag doll. I couldn't keep up with the names of all these positions. My PUSSY exploded. I couldn't stop cumming. Steven kept giving it to me. I didn't want to tap out. I wanted to show him I was a big girl, and I could hang, but damn those long strokes, I couldn't take it, but no I can't give up. It was getting so good a tear came out of my eye. My body trembled like an earthquake. "Oh, I'm cumming again Steven, again." "Oh, Oh," Steven stated shaking and I could feel his big, long dick get harder and harder inside of me. "Oh, shit, oh shit." "What baby, what Steven?" I said. "I'm cumming baby." He said as he slapped my big ass and he said. "Cum with me baby." He stroked me in rhythm. "Cum with me baby." He said and he smacked my ass in the right spot and there I go again, trembling and shaking and cumming all over the damn place until my side of the bed was soaking wet. Steven came so hard that I could feel his dick throbbing inside of me. Then we just lay on the bed trying to gain our composure.

After our breathing returned to normal, I turned to Steven and said, "Listen, you don't need to disappear, because I am not rushing you to get into a relationship." He lay there quietly listening to me. "What you and I have is special and I don't want to mess it up." "I feel the same way about Valencia, so where do we go from here?" "I am really feeling you now." I looked at Steven and said, "We can be Friends with Benefits." The look on his face was priceless. What did he expect? And what did you all expect?

CHAPTER TWELVE

Chatting With My Girls

After that night Steven called me every day. He would text me fifty times a day. Sometimes, I would just ignore them. It wasn't like I didn't like him, but I thought he should get a taste of his own medicine. I stared off into space for a few seconds and I envisioned Steven giving it to my big ass. I could hear the smacks on my ass as he was delivering all that good dick.

As I was thinking and having flashbacks, I could feel a warm sensation between my legs and my PUSSY started pulsating like crazy. The only thing that stopped me from going to get one of my toys for release was that the phone was ringing. It was Tamara with her crazy self. "Hello Valencia, what have you been doing?" "Nothing much Tamara, what about yourself?" "Nothing just sitting at home being bored." "Bored, Tamara you just need some dick in your life." "Yes, I do." We giggled. "So, have you talked to your little friend yet?" "No, not yet, and I haven't heard from him either." I had to tell her that, because I didn't want her in my business, then she and Rachael would clown on me. "Valencia, don't worry you will find another man who knows your worth, shit, you deserve a good man." "Thank you and you deserve to stop fucking old man Joe." "Whatever, that's why Joe gave me $1,000 dollars the other week and told me to go shopping." "Is that right?" "Don't knock it until you try it." "Tamara, I don't fuck old men, I just can't do it." "Okay, I will do it for you, while you keep chasing those young ass little boys, who you're having a hard time catching up with." "Now you want to go there huh?"

Then I heard my three-way line beep in. "Tamara, I have to answer the other line, I will call you back." I hung up the phone and answered the other line. "Hello Valencia, what's going on?" "Nothing, I just got off the phone with Tamara." "Oh, that's why she didn't answer her phone." "I guess so, she was too busy trying to get me hooked up with some dick, and she was talking about what I deserve." Rachael started laughing hard. "Oh really, that's why her trifling ass fuck old man Joe." I burst out laughing. "That girl is a damn trip. "Guess what she told me the other day Valencia?" "What did she tell you?" "She said his dick couldn't get up, and she tried sucking on it first, and it still wouldn't get up." Rachael snickered. "So, what happened?" "She said he ran outside to his truck to get his dick pump."

We both burst out laughing. I had to hold my stomach; I swear that had me in tears. After about four minutes of laughter, I had to stop, it felt like I had to piss on my damn self. "Okay, Rachael enough, enough." "Damn, you started it." "No, I didn't. "All right, so have you talked to that guy Steven yet?" "Can you keep a secret?" "Yes, you know I can girl." "I'm serious, I didn't tell Tamara, but he's been calling and texting me." "Valencia your secrets will stay with me, I won't say a word, and what did he have to say?" "I can't lie, he was in the club that night, but y'all didn't see him, and he came by my place after the club." "Say what, you little nasty hussy and you didn't let me know?" "I'm letting you know now." "You know what I'm talking about, then what happened?" "He came over and that's it." "That's it, Valencia who in the hell do you think you're fooling, he hit that ass didn't he?" I laughed. "Girl, he tore my PUSSY up, he had me waking bow-legged and shit." "Listen to you with your little nasty ass, you like him, don't you?" "Yeah, I do, but I'm not going to act thirsty and fall at his feet, so he can play me like a damn fool." "I hear you, girl, I hear you." "Do you know what I'm saying?" "Yes, I know exactly what you're saying." "Okay, let's keep this conversation between you and me." "You have my word, and are we going out this weekend?" Yes, I need to do some shopping." "Yeah, me too, talk to you later Valencia." "Bye."

CHAPTER THIRTEEN

I Finally Talked To Steven

I let Steven chase me for a few more days, and I finally answered the phone. "Hello, Valencia, you know you play too much." "What do you mean Steven?" "I know you were only trying to give me a taste of my own medicine." "Now why would I do that?" "Never mind, so what have you been up to?" 'I have been staying busy that's all." "You're too funny, I know you saw my calls and texts, but that's all right." "Again, why would I do that?" "That's okay I guess I deserved it, so are you going out this weekend?" "Yes, that's the plan." "Well, can I see you before then?" Damn, my PUSSY started pulsating. I thought I was the one in charge here.

The more Steven talked the more my PUSSY listened, and I started to get hypnotized. "Yes, sure we can see each other before then." Damn, I was trying to be hard, but now I want something hard. "When do you want me to come over?" "Damn, did you just say cum, Steven?" My PUSSY started to jump and do a hurdle, shit I'm horny now. I started stumbling with my words. "I, I, I will let you know later on this evening, okay?" "Okay, that sounds good." Damn, I am really feeling this guy. Is it the way he touches me, talks to me, or the way he fucked the shit out of me? I can't explain what he does to my spirit. I feel tranquil when I'm with him. I truly hope Steven doesn't have any hidden agenda.

As far as I am concerned, I cannot have my heart broken again. I was being serious with myself, then I felt a little soggy between my legs. I think I'd better tell Steven to get his ass over here as soon as possible. My PUSSY needs a beat down badly. So, I called Steven back and told him to come over on hump day, which we all know is Wednesday. Shit, they don't call it that for anything. I am wet and I am ready to hump! I could tell he was happy. He agreed. I must admit, I was happy too. I was all excited until my phone rang. "Hello, who is this?" "Hey Valencia, this is Tamara." "Hey, Tamara, what's wrong?" "Why didn't your ass tell me you still seeing Steven, and he came over and put it on your ass?" I was stunned for a second. "Girl, who told you?" I knew damn well Rachael told her because I didn't tell anyone else. Didn't she promise she wouldn't say anything? "I didn't want to tell you, because I knew you would clown me about it." "Valencia, you are my friend for life, please don't hide anything from me."

"Okay, okay, Tamara." "Now that we got the bullshit out of the way, did he tear that ass up again?" We both laughed. "You must really like this guy?" "Why do you say that?" "You lied to your girl about him, that dick must really have you sprung, but I'm not hating on you, to each his own." "Thank you, Tamara, I'm not trying to rush anything right now, we are still friends with benefits." "That's right take your damn time and then when you get the chance ride that dick like you're crazy and then put his ass in a buck and see how he likes it." "What girl?" We both started laughing. "You're so crazy Tamara." "I know I am, but guess what?" "What Tamara?" "I'm not talking to an old man Joe anymore." "Why is that?" "His old ass couldn't get it up even after I sucked his dick." I burst out laughing. "What's so funny?" "Rachael told me, he went and got a pump to pump up that old dick." "Say what?" "That heffa, I told her to keep that a secret." I chuckled. "Keep a secret?" "Her ass can't hold water." "Neither can you." We both just laughed. "The old guy couldn't do anything with you huh?" "Hell Knaw, his dick went on vacation, and I was just lying in the bed patting on my PUSSY." "Damn!

CHAPTER FOURTEEN

He Fucked Me Good

Wednesday finally came and I was very happy. I barely slept and I woke up wet as hell between my legs. It felt like Steven had just gotten out of my PUSSY. Damn, I could feel him all inside of me. I carried on with my day and then my phone rang. "Hello, Valencia, what time do you want me to come over?" "You can come over about 5 p.m." "That sounds good, I will see you then." "Okay don't forget to bring lots of raincoats." We both started laughing. "I won't forget."

CHARLES LEE ROBINSON JR.

When 5 p.m. came, I was all showered and I had everything ready to go. The music was ready, and the candles were lit. I found my long black trench coat and my black heels, and I was ready to rock Stevens's world. I had my body all shined up and I put the coat on with no underwear underneath. I was hot and I was ready for that dick. I was ready for seduction. The doorbell rang. I looked at the clock and Steven was right on time. My phone rang as I opened the door, but I didn't pay any attention. My PUSSY was hot, and she was pulsating. I didn't want to let him know that I was as excited as he was to see me. I played it cool. "Valencia why do you have that coat on with those shoes, girl it smells good in here." I curled my finger as if to tell him to follow me into the bedroom. That curling of the finger is something else, for some reason, it can really hypnotize a man. As soon as we made it to the bedroom, *I dropped the trench coat onto the floor. I could see Steven staring at my shiny curves from the body oil I put on. I kept my heels on and I slowly walked backwards to my bed. Steven followed with his hands on my hips. I laid down and I spread both legs wide open. Steven started kissing my inner thighs. His tongue was so hot that it slid up and down my legs. It felt so good. My body started getting goosebumps. Then his hands put my mind at ease. He rubbed on my breast and my nipples. I could feel my nipples; they were so hard and sensitive. A hot tongue started circling my areola. I looked up to watch the art that this man was displaying on my body. I started moaning loudly and every time he kissed and sucked on my body, I could hear him groaning as enjoyed it himself. The moment was so tense, the air felt still as he pleased every inch of my body. The gentle touch of his hands made me squirm. "Oh. Steven." "Yes, baby?" "Mmmmm, that feels so good. "Steven slowly turned me to my side and opened my legs and then he went face first with his tongue and soft lips. I could hear his lips and my lips making beautiful and succulent noises. I started to tremble and cum at the same time. "Put it in, baby please put it in." He leaned over and pulled a condom out of his pants pocket. Then he dropped his pants down to the floor. "I see you came prepared," I whispered. "Yes, I came prepared for all this ass." He whispered back. I felt his long and strong dick enter my sugar walls. I gripped the sheets, and my eyes rolled up inside my head. "Oh my, oh shit, oh, oh, ahhhh, damn it feels so damn good. "I started to tremble more. As Steven stroked me slowly, he kissed my neck and his hot tongue circled motions of desire and passion. I felt his hot breath all over me. Then his back got tense as his strokes got a little more speed. I grabbed for the pillows, sheets, air, and everything that I could possibly grip. The motion of his hips was incredible. I couldn't think, the only thing I could do was enjoy, and enjoy what I did. "Oh baby, I'm about to cum Steven." He stroked it and stroked it in every direction. "Let's cum together." He whispered in my ear. "Here it cums, here it cums, I'm cumming." Oh, Oh, Grrrrr, I'm cumming, too, baby." We both reached our climax at the same time. Oh, my goodness.*

CHAPTER FIFTEEN

No Hidden Agenda

After Steven rocked my world, we lay in bed until we got our composure back. I laid on his chest and we started chatting about some serious things. "So, are we going to stay friends with benefits Valencia?" "That all depends on what you want because I don't want to have feelings for someone who doesn't feel the same about me." "I understand that." "I can't have someone sexing me and disappearing." "You're right, and I don't plan on disappearing ever again. When I heard that, a big gulp or lump came into my throat. "So, what are you saying?" "I'm saying I want us to be exclusive." "Exclusive in what way?" "Oh, so you're making me spell it out?" "Do what you have to do bro." We both laughed. "I want you to be my woman." I smiled. "Let me get this straight, Playboy the love bug Steven, is ready to settle down with V?" "Yes, I am ready to settle down with you V, or Valencia." I giggled. "See I love that about you." "What do you love about me?" "I love how good you make me feel when we're making love and you make me laugh." "Guess what I like about you Steven?" "What's that?" "I love the way you throw that big, long, and strong dick inside me." We laughed. "With all seriousness, now you don't have any hidden agenda, you just want to be with only me, right?" "Valencia, I don't have No Hidden Agenda." "Good, because it's a done deal." Steven smiled and we started kissing passionately.

Next thing you know we were back at the lovemaking. My legs went up and the stroking and the moaning and the groaning began. Damn, I can't wait to tell my girls this. Oh, never mind they don't need to know. Ha, ha, Steven and I are now a couple, we both are ready, we are!

THE END!!!

CHARLES LEE ROBINSON JR.

RELATIONSHIPS TODAY
THE UPS & DOWNS AND THE UGLY TRUTH

CHARLES LEE ROBINSON JR.

RELATIONSHIPS
TODAY

THE UPS & DOWNS AND THE UGLY TRUTH

WRITTEN BY
CHARLES LEE ROBINSON JR.

CHARLES LEE ROBINSON JR.

IN THIS BOOK, I PUT TOGETHER SEVEN DIFFERENT STORIES OF RELATIONSHIPS THAT YOU MAY BE ABLE TO RELATE TO!

Each book will take you on a rollercoaster ride of life, with intense drama, heartbreak, retaliation, and suspense!

SINGLE BY CHOICE

WHAT MOTIVATES A MAN TO LOVE HIS WOMAN

MY BODY WANT SEX BUT MY HEART WANTS LOVE

SOMETIMES, A MAN JUST WANTS PEACE

JUST TO SAY I GOT A MAN

LOVE DOESN'T HAVE A NAME

FRIENDS WITH BENEFITS

CHARLES LEE ROBINSON JR.

CASUAL COMFORT PRODUCTIONS

THE UPS & DOWNS AND THE UGLY TRUTH:

On my journey to write books about relationships with joy, pain, sorrow, commitment, infidelity, love, and hate, I always get the same question repeatedly and that's "Why do I write these books?" The answer is always the same, it's my purpose to educate those who have questions and those who want to be healed from devastating endings to relationships that they thought would last them a lifetime.

Toxic people and toxic relationships are now a part of our culture and it's a shame when two adults cannot talk things out and try to find the root of the problem so they can fix their relationship and restore it.

The ugly truth is that many of us aren't healed from our past and we keep bringing old baggage from our past relationships, Whether Man or Woman we all have faults and that's something many of us aren't willing to admit. We don't take accountability for our part in the situations and we don't see ourselves as being one part of the break-up.

SELF-SABOTOGE: Self-sabotaging your relationship is a real problem that we need to address. Have you ever gotten into a relationship you thought was too good to be true? Don't think that way because you are opening up the doors to self-sabotaging yourself. Don't do it!

Relationships

Today

THE UPS & DOWNS AND THE UGLY TRUTH

WRITTEN BY

CHARLES LEE ROBINSON JR.

CHARLES LEE ROBINSON JR.

PURCHASE LINK:

amazon.com/author/robinsonc

Made in the USA
Columbia, SC
30 September 2023